PAID

PAID

A Guide to Credit and Collections for Canadian Business Owners

IAN FEARON CCE, CCP

iUniverse, Inc.
Bloomington

PAID
A Guide to Credit and Collections for Canadian Business Owners

iUniverse books may be ordered through booksellers or by contacting:

iUniverse
1663 Liberty Drive
Bloomington, IN 47403
www.iuniverse.com
1-800-Authors (1-800-288-4677)

ISBN: 978-1-4620-3612-7 (sc)
ISBN: 978-1-4620-3613-4 (ebk)

Printed in the United States of America

iUniverse rev. date: 08/10/2011

Introduction

For over 30 years I managed the Credit and Accounts Receivable departments of some of the largest corporations in the world; Phillip Morris Co., Tech Data, Motorola and Hitachi to name a few. Over the years I have managed over $10 Billion (no that's not a misprint) in revenues with bad debt write offs of less than $2 million. That's 0.02% of sales.

During that time I collected from public and private companies, from members of organized crime, from companies that claimed to be bankrupt and in one case at the wrong end of a loaded handgun.

I've taught these techniques to hundreds of companies from Shanghai to San Diego, at Community Colleges and Co-Op Programs. In short, my methods work. Not only do I get paid, but I keep the customer as a business partner. In this guide, I share my experiences in an easy to understand format. I have personally used each and every technique at least once.

I recently left the corporate world to offer my services to the Small, Medium Business (SMB) owners who don't have and probably don't need a full time credit and collection staff. In sharing my experience, I have taken three approaches, each of which compliments the other; Consulting through Onsite Credit Group (www.onsitecreditgroup.com) Software to enhance receivable management through www.simplypaid.ca (under development) And this Guide to Credit and Collections for Business Owners

As a business owner, you have a lot of responsibilities. Getting paid on time shouldn't be one of them. If you're granting terms to your customers, you are in effect giving them an interest free loan until they pay you for your product or services. If you get paid late, your profit margins will be less. If you don't get paid at all, the consequences can be significant. I've seen a lot of companies go out of business because they lost focus on receivables.

Whenever possible, I've provided both a simplified and a comprehensive recommendation. Please feel free to choose the one that works best for you or combine both.

By following this guide, you will improve your cash flow, increase your profits and free yourself up to grow your business. The guide is meant to be used as you need it. You can follow it from the beginning through to the end or you can refer to different topics as needed. When applicable, I've added a template for you to use in setting up your own credit and collection functions. I've tried to keep the book enjoyable as well as educational. I share some of my experiences which hopefully you will find valuable.

Most of all "Profit From My Experience."

This guide is divided into 5 primary sections;

1. An assessment of your current credit operations
2. Risk Management which includes opening and investigating new accounts, setting and reviewing credit limit
3. Receivables Management which includes collection of accounts receivable
4. Tips & Tricks to guide you through the credit and collection process
5. Appendix which includes sample forms, policies and a set of templates

SECTION 1

Assessment of Current Credit Operations

Procedure and Policy

Collection Process

Security

First Things First

Whenever a new client hires me to consult with them, I start the process with a review of their current procedures and policies. The following questionnaire covers most of that review process. We'll cover each aspect in depth later in this guide. For now, please take the time to complete the questions so that you can assess your relative strengths and areas we can improve on.

Procedure and Policy

		Yes	No
1a	Is there a written credit and collection policy and procedure?		
1b	Does everyone involved (i.e. Sales and Service) have a copy of the procedure?		
1c	Is there a formal credit application?		
1d	Is the credit application signed?		
1e	Does the application include a tax exemption certificate?		
1f	Are the terms stated on the credit application?		
1g	Is there a title retention clause?		
1h	Does the application include an authorization clause?		
1i	Is a second signature required to approve credit above a specific level?		
1j	Is there a maximum allowed without financial statements?		
1k	Is there a late payment or interest clause?		
1l	Does the application include a clause regarding cash application?		
1m	Who approves new accounts? (enter titles, not names)		
1n	What is each person's approval level?		
1o	How is the applicant verified? (to prevent fraud)		
1p	What information is used to open new accounts?		
1q	What is the current source of credit information?		
1r	Notes:		

Collections Process

2	What is the average DSO/What should it be?	Yes	No
		Yes	**No**
2a	Is there a regular aging run?		
2b	Is there a formal collection process in place?		
2c	Are customer statements sent out?		
2d	Is the current collection process adequate?		
2e	How many accounts are active?		
2f	How many staff are currently working on active collections?		
2g	Is sales staff responsible for collections?		
2h	Are the terms stated on the invoice?		
2i	Are invoices sent out on a timely basis?		
2j	Are payments applied as received?		
2k	Do customer statements show open items or balance forward?		
2l	Do the statements clearly show the past due amounts?		
2m	Are extended terms/deferred terms invoices shown in the total A/R?		
2n	Are extended terms included as part of the credit limit?		
2o	Is it easy to reprint invoices?		
2p	Do customers provide purchase orders?		
2q	If so, where are the original purchase orders stored?		
2r	Who is responsible for collections? (use titles, not names)		
2s	What training and background does the person have?		
2t	How are collections being made? (see SimplyPaid.ca)		

Notes:
DSO is calculated by dividing the total annual sales by 365
to produce an average daily sales
The average daily sales is then divided into the closing A/R
to provide a Days' Sales Outstanding (DSO)

Security

			Yes	No
3	What determines when a customer needs to provide security?			
			Yes	**No**
3a	Is there a standard security agreement available?			
3b	Is the original stored safely?			
3c	Who files any security agreements?			
3d	Are personal guarantees used in lieu of equity?			
	Third Party/Legal		**Yes**	**No**
3e	Is there a third party collection agent in place?			
	What rates are being charged?			
			Yes	**No**
3f	Are the rates competitive?			
3g	Will the collection agent sue or refer the file to outside council?			
3h	Is there outside council available and if so do they understand the business?			
3i	Are proofs of claim routinely filed and are they filed correctly?			
3j	What was the bad debt rate for the last 3 years?			
			Yes	**No**
3k	Is a reserve routinely set?			
3l	If so, when, how and by whom?			

Your Responses and What They Mean

1a.

I recommend that you prepare and distribute a written credit and collection policy. The policy doesn't have to be a lengthy document. An internal memo or email will do. I have included a policy template in the appendix which you can use to write your own document. Your policy should state who has what authority and what processes are followed.

1b.

Everyone in your organization that deals with customers should have a copy of your credit and collection policy. Everyone should give the customer the same answer if the customer asks about your policies. If the customer gets a different answer from one person than another, that will undermine your policy and may give the customer a reason not to pay you on time.

1c, 1d.

The credit application is a key document for doing business with your customers. It covers most of the credit basics that you need in order to make informed decisions. A written and signed credit application is a legal binding document between you and your new customer. I'll discuss the application in detail later and we'll use a template to help you through the process but for now, make it a policy to never open a new account without a signed credit application.

1e

Although at the time of this writing, there are no exemptions for most goods and services within Canada, your application should include a spot where the customer can enter an exemption number just in case the various levels of government decide to change the rules. It's easier to have a space that isn't used than it is to reprint your application and we all know how often the tax rules change.

1f.

Your credit application should state your standard terms of sale (or that the terms are stated on the invoice) in case of any dispute. When the customer applies for credit with you, he is agreeing to your terms. He may later claim that his standard terms are different than what is on the invoice and in the case of a disagreement you can show him the credit application that he signed.

1g

As an unsecured supplier you are at risk of not getting paid if your customer becomes insolvent and can't pay his suppliers. There is a way to make sure that you do get paid ahead of everyone else, including the bank. We'll discuss that later. For now I would add a clause to your credit application that says you retain title to your product (we'll talk about services later).

1h

Your credit application should include a clause that states that the person signing the application has the authority to sign on behalf of the company. This is your assurance that the person who signs the application is allowed to enter into a legal agreement that you will be paid for your product or services.

1i.

I recommend that there be a requirement within your credit policy that a second signature is required before granting a credit limit in excess of a specific amount. The amount will vary depending on the ability and training of the primary credit granter, but as a safe measure I recommend that a second signature be required at some point in the credit granting process.

1j.

Unless you have some form of security, you are always at risk when you grant credit terms. You want to limit your risk as much as possible and you never want to have more of your money at risk than the owners of the company you are granting credit to. The best way to assess the risk is to ask for a copy of the customer's financial statement. If you can get the financials; excellent, otherwise you have to find out as much as you can without them. I'll show you how to do that later.

1k.

Your credit application should include an interest clause on past due invoices and the interest rate should be high enough so that the customer does not use your company as a source of financing instead of the bank

1l.

Your credit application should include a clause that gives you the right to apply payments as you see fit and not based on some arbitrary process. This is especially true if you charge interest on past due invoices.

1m

When setting up your policy, use titles, not names so that if the person in the position changes, you don't have to change your policy.

1n.

I recommend that you have approval levels that are clearly set out for anyone involved in granting credit. This makes sure that credit limits are properly approved and maintained.

1o.

Do not open a new account unless you are able to confirm the legal name either yourself or through one of the reporting agencies or your banker.

1p.

Before opening any new account, you should have all of the information you need to make an informed decision. I'll go over the importance of each section when we look at the sample credit application.

1q

The two main sources of credit reports in Canada are Dun & Bradstreet and Equifax. Both have valuable information and both have advantages over the other. I show you how to read both reports later. I'll also look at a new source of information that has just become available in Canada.

2.

How do you know if you are collecting your money as quickly as possible without restricting sales? The most common measurement used in called Days Sales Outstanding (DSO). I cover DSO in depth later.

2a.

It's almost impossible to effectively collect outstanding accounts receivable without knowing which customers have paid. Running a regular aging report can highlight which accounts are past due and should be called for payment. I suggest running an aging at the beginning of each month. You should note any customers who are past due and phone, fax or email the customer for a payment.

I cover collections extensively later.

2b.

A formal collection process is important to manage cash flow and make sure customers pay within terms. Some customers will only pay when collection calls are made because they are managing their own cash flow. You don't want to provide interest free financing to your customers, therefore you need a collection process that will remind customers when to pay. The process doesn't have to be complicated; it could be as simple as calling the customer as a friendly reminder.

2c.

A lot of SMB don't send statements arguing that the mailing costs are too high. You need to consider the cost of giving the customer free financing compared to the cost of a stamp. If you can fax or email the statement that will save you the postage costs.

2d.

Measuring the effectiveness of your collection process is subjective. Some suppliers get paid more quickly than others and some suppliers don't get paid at all. If you're getting paid in less than 1.5 times your net terms (see 2 above) and you have less than 1% over 90 days, you have an effective collection process. If not, don't worry I'll help you get there.

2e, 2f

The number of active accounts will help determine how many resources you need to assign to collections. Resources include both people and systems. For now, please list the number of accounts that have an open balance and the number of people that actively contact customers for payment. I'll give you a staffing guideline later.

2g

It may be a conflict for sales to be involved with collections. The sales person also has the responsibility for making a sale to the same customer and may sacrifice collections in exchange for a large order. If this process has been effective for you in the past, it may be OK to continue but I suggest that you monitor it closely.

2h

The terms of sale should be clearly stated on your invoice. Combined with the credit application, this should help you to resolve any disputes with the customer.

2i

Before I consulted with them, some of my clients saved up invoices and mailed them once or twice per week. When you do that, you are delaying payment since customers generally pay after receiving an invoice regardless of when they received the product or service.

2j

It might seem cost effective to deposit customer cheques daily* but apply payments once a week or once a month. Although the money is in the bank, you have no way of monitoring past due accounts or customers that are over limit.

(*hopefully you are making regular bank deposits, if not daily at least twice per week)

2k

Open item statements are much easier to reconcile than balance forward statements. Both are acceptable but this guide deals only with open items.

2l

Your statement should show any past due invoices both in detail and in aging columns or buckets. Many of your customers only consider that they have to pay past due invoices and not invoices that are just becoming due. This will impact your cash flow.

2m, 2n

Any extended or deferred terms invoices should show on the statement even if the invoice is not due. You must also include any deferred invoices in the credit limit you have given the customer.

2o

One delaying tactics most often used by customers is to ask for a copy of an invoice. We'll talk a lot about this in the collection section. For now, you need to make sure that it's easy to reprint invoices. Whatever software you use should be able to produce invoices in both a hard copy and a soft copy format (i.e. pdf). If you invoice manually, make sure you keep a copy.

2p, 2q

It may be your business practise to accept verbal purchase orders from some or all customers. My experience has been that this is often a point of concern. If you do require written purchase orders, make sure you store the original safely in case of a dispute.

Even if it is your policy to accept verbal purchase orders, I suggest you ask for a fax or email confirmation especially for large orders.

2r, 2s, 2t

Whoever is responsible for collecting your receivables has your cash flow in their hands. Unless they have proper training, you could be putting yourself at risk.

I can't make a Credit Manager out of your staff, but this guide will make sure that he or she is effective. If you are responsible yourself, I'll help you to balance the need to make the sale and the need to get paid.

I'll show you how to make collections calls and then I'll offer you the choice of having most of it done automatically for you.

3

Regardless of what products or services you provide, there is a maximum amount you should allow your customers to owe you without some kind of guarantee that you will be paid. As we will see when we look at the true costs of bad debt, the more the customer owes you, the higher the risk you are taking on.

If you haven't considered this point yet, please leave it blank.

3, 3b, 3c

If you have a security agreement, it should have standard terms and conditions. I have provided a standard agreement in the appendix. Once you have a standard agreement in place you should store it in a fireproof storage cabinet since you may need to rely on the original in case of a dispute. You cannot sue to recover your account without the original agreement.

If you're not sure about the filing, ask your banker or accountant to provide you with a safe storage.

3d.

Personal guarantees are hard to enforce since you don't know who else has the same guarantee. If the owners of the company did not invest enough money in the company to make sure it was viable, then you should reconsider granting credit terms.

3e, 3f, 3g, 3h

If you have to submit an account to a collection agency, you should find one that charges a competitive fee and one that will work with you. The agency should allow you a free 10 day demand period. The agent should have an in house legal staff.

I'll discuss collection agencies later.

3i

Even if your customer goes into bankruptcy, there is often money to be repaid to the trade creditors at the end of the filing. Many suppliers don't file proofs of claim either because they think they won't get any payment, think they need a lawyer or because they don't know how to file a claim.

I cover the Bankruptcy Act and proofs of claim in later sections.

3k, l

To avoid cash flow problems, you will need to set a reserve for doubtful accounts. Your accountants will insist that you set a reserve and they will question how you set the amounts. I'll show you how and when to set your reserve

Now that we have a snap shot of your current processes, let's look at how to improve those areas that can increase your cash flow and make you some more money.

SECTION 2

Risk Management

Role of the Credit Department

Procedure and Policy

Credit Applications

Third Party Reports

Banks and Bank References

Personal Guarantees

Types of Businesses in Canada

Welcome Letters

Minimizing Your Risk

Credit Insurance

Factoring Receivables

Export Development Corporation

Bank and Corporate Guarantees

Setting Credit Limits Over $25,000

Alternate Sources of Financial Information

Financial Analysis

Selling Services on Credit

Role of the Credit Department

Whether you're a manufacturer, a reseller or a service provider, your credit department should play a key role in your business model. Whether you have a formal, structured department or you share the responsibilities among yourself and your staff, the credit department must add value to your organization.

I've been called a lot of names by people that don't understand my role and function. I've been called the Credit Police, The Anti-Sales Department, Doctor No and my favourite Interfearon. At the end of the day however I've gained the respect of my detractors by adding value to any organization I've worked with because I take the position that the credit department has to be a business partner to both the internal and the external customer.

It's my job to find a way to make every sale that comes across my desk. I can't always give credit terms and sometimes I have to insist on cash before shipping but I'm not adding value if I simply say no. I can write a computer program that does that and I expect that you could as well

As we look at the process of granting credit and collecting please keep in mind that your credit department is a key part of your business.

Procedure and Policy

A Simplified Process

It is extremely important that you have a written procedure and policy and that everyone in your company who deals with your customers has a copy. The procedure and policy is like the foundation of a building. If the foundation isn't strong, it won't stand up to the business stress and strain. If you and your staff don't have a process to follow, you will eventually make the wrong decisions.

I found out very early in my consulting practice that SMB owners often sell based on relationships. You may know your customer personally and be confident that he's going to pay you. However, it's not he that owes you the money; it's his company which is the same as selling to a third party.

A simplified procedure and policy can be as short as an internal memo or email something like;

"It is the policy of the company to grant credit only to customers who complete and submit the company's credit application. Only the Owner is authorized to approve credit terms to customers."

I don't suggest using this simplified method to grant any more than $5-10,000.

Setting & Revising Limits Using A Simplified Procedure and policy;

1. Get a completed and signed credit application.
2. Confirm the correct legal name of your customer either from the company itself or sources like the internet.
3. Call the 3 references on the credit application. If they provide a good reference, take the average of their credit limits and use that as a guideline.
4. Open the account, give it a credit limit and start selling.
5. If the customer does not pay on time, call their accounts payable department. If you still don't get paid, put new orders on hold until the account is current.
6. If the customer won't or can't pay you then turn the account over to a collection agent when the oldest invoice is 60 days past the due date.
7. Write off any bad debts on a regular basis.

Modified Process;

In addition to the above steps, I would suggest that you give every customer a risk code of Low, Medium or High. You can code your accounts either manually or within whatever software you use to process your orders.

A low risk customer is a customer who pays you on time. All orders can be approved up to the credit limit whether there are past due invoices or not.

A medium risk customer is a customer who pays you late but not more than twice your terms of sale. All orders will be approved up to the credit limit unless there are past due invoices. If there are past due invoices, the customer must be contacted for payment before new orders are released. If the customer has a track record of paying more or less on time, then new orders can be released based on a promise to pay.

A high risk customer is a customer who can't or won't pay you on time. Regardless of how much the customer owes or whether there are past due invoices or not, all orders must be manually approved. This method is time consuming but if your customer has a track record of not paying you on time, it's the best way to manage your exposure.

Use a combination of the credit limit and the risk code to manage your credit limits. Gradually increase limits for low risk customer; keep medium customers within the credit limit and more or less current. Be very firm in not allowing high risk customers to owe you for more than one order at a time

Setting and Revising Limits Using A Comprehensive Policy;

If you grant large lines of unsecured credit, if your gross profit margins are low or if you have the resources, a comprehensive credit granting process may prove to be the best model for you to follow.

A comprehensive procedure and policy might look like the one in the appendix. I have outlined how to use the two primary sources of credit information, Dun & Bradstreet and Equifax to set and revise credit limits. The draft policy should give you enough guidelines to approve up to $25,000 at which point I would recommend either securing your account through an inventory security agreement (see the sample ISA in the appendix) or at least requesting a financial statement from your customer. I'll discuss financial statements later in the guide.

Regardless of which method you use, here are the most important points for you to consider when writing and distributing your policy;

- it is an excellent training tool for new employees
- it provides a guideline for making credit decisions that are fair and consistent to all customers
- it provides excellent support for employees to explain credit and collection decisions
- it provides documentation to your bank that procedures and policies are in place

Your policy should state who has what authority and what processes are followed. As the business owner, you have the right to overrule your policies and you can often use this approach to resolve issues with customers. For example your written policy may state that you don't ship new orders to customers that are past due. Your staff should follow that policy but if the customer appeals the decision to you as the owner, you can always approve the order while supporting your staff by making an exception to the policy. I would recommend that you only make an exception in exchange for a commitment from the customer to bring the account current.

I have a point that I'd like to make here. It is important that if your staff follows the policy and puts an account on hold or declines a credit limit increase and you make an executive decision to overrule policy that you reassure your staff that they did the right thing by following policy. That way they don't think you are overruling *them*. My practice has always been to let my staff advise the customer that their order will be approved or the limit increased even if the decision is made by the business owner. If the customer thinks he can bypass your staff and deal directly with you, you run the risk of your staff becoming ineffective. The staff does not have to agree with you, but they deserve the right to be advised of your decision. Letting them advise the customer reinforces the relationship they have with him/her.

Your banker will be pleased to know that you have a policy in place because it reassures him that you are managing your risks. Bankers like predictability and he probably will add a copy of your policy to his loan file.

Everyone in your organization that deals with customers should have a copy of your credit and collection policy and everyone in your organization should give the customer the same answer if he asks about your policy. If the customer gets a different answer from one person than another, that will undermine your policy and may give the customer a reason not to pay you on time.

This includes sales and customer service. The Sales staff has the most interaction with your customers so they need to know if there is a credit problem. If Sales is aware of the policy they can often help to bring the customer current so that they can take new orders. There is nothing worse for a salesman than finding out that his customer is on hold especially if he finds that out from the customer himself. If the salesman knows what the policy is and is kept informed, then he should understand that every customer is treated the same. At the same time, the Sales staff must understand that policy has to be followed. Letting Sales staff make credit decisions can be a conflict of interest.

The shipping department should know if your policy is not to ship to past due accounts. Quite often, the customer will contact the shipper and try to convince them to ship whatever has been ordered. If the shipper does not know the policy, he may think the customer is making a reasonable request and go ahead and ship, especially if the customer is well known. Customers who pick up orders present the greatest risk since they will try to convince the shipper that there is no problem with his account and that he needs the product now, not after the credit department approves the order. (beware of the "Gotta Have" which I'll discuss later).

I recommend that there be a requirement within your credit policy that a second signature is needed before granting a credit limit in excess of a specific amount. The amount will vary depending on the ability and training of the primary credit granter, but as a safe measure I recommend that a second signature be required at some point in the credit granting process. This allows for management to have proper controls in place. Your bank may assist in this aspect of your credit policy since they are loaning you money against future receivables and will want to see proper controls in place. I strongly suggest that you have a formal procedure in place. For example, you could allow the office manager to approve up to $10,000 and limits above that require the approval of the owner. This makes sure that you have the opportunity of setting the limit on an account and assessing the risk. After all, when you extend credit terms to your customers, you are giving them an interest free loan until you are paid. You want to make sure that not only do you get paid, but that you get paid on time.

I do not recommend that Sales staff set credit limits since it is a conflict of interest. I do however recommend that Sales staff participate in the process.

When setting up your policy, use titles, not names so that if the person in the position changes, you don't have to change your policy. For example, if Tom the office manager is responsible for approving orders up to $10,000 use the title "Office Manager" and not the name "Tom." If Tom retires, you don't have to rewrite your policy.

Revisit your procedure and policy from time to time. The business environment is constantly changing. You may need to amend your policy to make sure you aren't putting yourself at risk or missing out on sales opportunities.

Credit Applications

In the introduction I mentioned that where possible I would provide both a Simplified and a Comprehensive process. ***There is no simple process when it comes to credit applications.***

The credit application establishes legal liability, the terms and conditions under which you grant terms, what the consequences are for not paying you on time and helps you to determine how much, if any credit to grant. If you get the credit application completely and factually completed then you will have less problems getting paid. Credit managers like to say that a properly opened account is 90% collected.

Because there are no shortcuts for getting the credit application completed and signed, I have included my template in the appendix. It's been tested over 30 years and thousands of accounts. It's been challenged by many lawyers and stood up to all kinds of law suits. It works; make changes to it at your own risk.

The credit application is a key document for doing business with your customers. It covers most of the credit basics that you need to make informed decisions. A written and signed credit application is a legal binding document between you and your new customer. It legally binds the customer to pay you if you grant credit terms. The credit application gives you permission to conduct a credit investigation. This is especially important if you are granting credit to a sole proprietorship or a partnership. The credit application will also identify the legal entity that you are selling to. If you invoice incorrectly or if you invoice a customer that has not applied for credit, you may have difficulty getting paid. A properly completed credit application will also help you to locate the customer if he moves without paying you since he has given you the names of other suppliers as well as his bank. Collection agents and skip tracers rely on this information to recover your money.

Never open a new account without a credit application. If you receive an application that is not signed, return it to the customer and insist on a signature. It's acceptable for the customer to give you bank and trade references on a separate page and state on the application "see attached" but unless the application is signed, do not proceed any further. If you get an application that says "see attached" in the legal name field, send it back. There is no such company as "see attached." It is also important that the person who signs the application has the authority to bind the company; otherwise liability can be denied. You don't need an original signature. The Courts will accept an electronic signature since that's how most business is conducted. A faxed credit application is acceptable

Before opening any new account, you should have the following information from the credit application;

- the legal name of the company (this may be different than the doing business as name)
- the trade style or doing business as name
- the legal street address where you're going to send your invoices to
- the ship to address if different than the address you're sending invoices to
- the name, branch and phone number of the customer's bank
- the name and address of at least 2 and preferably 3 suppliers
- the name and phone number of the person who will pay the invoices (I also recommend that you have an email address)

Although at the time of this writing, there are no exemptions for most goods and services within Canada, your application should include a spot where the customer can enter an exemption number just in case the various levels of government decide to change the rules. It's easier to have a space that isn't used than it is to reprint your application and we all know how often the tax rules change. If you sell your product or services to U.S. customers you will need a state tax exemption certificate called a W9 or you will be liable for the taxes.

Your credit application should state that your standard terms of sale are on your invoices in case of any dispute. When the customer applies for credit with you, he is agreeing to your terms. He may later claim that his standard terms are different than what is on the invoice and in the case of a disagreement you can show him the credit application that he signed.

We'll talk later about the terms on the customers' purchase orders being different from your standard terms but for now, I strongly recommend that you include your terms on the application. I have often had a conversation with a customer who claims he was given terms that are different than those stated on the application. At the end of the day, you can rely on the application to support your terms. Notice clause 6 under terms and conditions.

Your standard terms are exactly that, your normal terms of sale. That does not mean that you can't offer different terms at different times for different reasons (for example seasonal terms or extended terms when you introduce a new product or service. However, you must legally treat "like customers alike." By having your standard terms on the application you can avoid any claims of preferential treatment. We'll talk about preference in another section.

As an unsecured supplier you are at risk of not getting paid if your customer becomes insolvent and can't pay his suppliers. There is a way to make sure that you do get paid ahead of everyone else, including the bank. We'll discuss that later. For now I would add a clause to your credit application that says you retain title to your product (we'll talk about services later). The title retention clause is included in the sample credit application in the appendix. In the case of a legal dispute, you can't rely entirely on this clause but you can use it as "moral suasion" when dealing with a past due account. If you point out to the customer that he does not own the product until he pays you, you may be able to get paid or if you prefer, take the product back. Be aware that there are some risks in taking product back but I would rather that you argue from a position of strength. I'd rather you had the product back than leave it with the customer.

Your credit application should include a clause that states that the person signing the application has the authority to sign on behalf of the company. This is your assurance that the person who signs the application is allowed to enter into a legal agreement that you will be paid for your product or services. The customer can't deny that they agreed to pay you since they applied for credit.

Attaching a void cheque is useful even if you don't use a lockbox since it helps you to locate the customer's money if he doesn't pay you. Keep a copy of the void cheque in your credit file.

You want the customer to confirm the type of business he's running and the size of his location. If you're shipping pallet loads of product into an 800 square foot retail store you're going to have problems. I cover the types of business later.

You want to know how long the business has been in operations since new companies may fail with the first 5 years. If you can't confirm how long the business has been in operation, treat it as less than 1 year old.

If the company has branches or if you're shipping product somewhere other than head office, you need to know the address in case you need to get your product back. If the customer uses an outside or third party warehouse you need to know where the product is. If someone other than the business owns the warehouse then you may be at risk if your customer does not pay the landlord. If you secure your account with an Inventory Security Agreement you'll want to know where your inventory is at all times.

Some customers will try to avoid paying you by stating that the person that signed the application was not authorized to do so. You don't have to prove whether or not that is true. You accepted the signature as being approval and the company has a responsibility to honour its commitments. If all else fails, you can sue the person who signed the application for fraudulent misrepresentation. In my career I have never had a company deny liability based on who signed the application.

Your credit application should include an interest clause on past due invoices and the interest rate should be high enough so that the customer does not use your company as a source of financing instead of the bank. In the case of a dispute you may be able to recover your account in full plus interest if the customer agrees to the interest clause. If the customer is having problems paying you in future, you can always offer to waive the interest if you receive payment of the principal amount; however you can't charge interest unless the customer is advised first and agrees to the conditions and the rates.

If you have customers who tell you that they will pay the interest penalty but not the invoice amounts, that's a very clear warning sign since it means that they can't pay the principle amount they owe you and can't borrow any more money from their bank to avoid your interest penalty. If you have such customers, put them on hold immediately. I suggest that you charge 1.5% interest per month which is 18% per year.

Your credit application should include a clause that gives you the right to apply payments as you see fit and not based on some arbitrary process. This is especially true if you charge interest on past due invoices. Without this clause, the customer can dispute the balance that you claim as past due by making the argument that you applied the payments to the wrong invoices. It can also create reconciliation problems in future.

Do not open a new account unless you are able to confirm the legal name either yourself or through one of the reporting agencies such as Dun & Bradstreet or Equifax. Most frauds occur because the supplier did not conduct a proper credit investigation. Most credit reporting companies charge a reasonable fee to conduct the investigation for you. If the information in the credit report does not agree with the credit application, check out the facts before opening the account.

Your bank may also be able to provide you with a credit report on a new customer or at least confirm that you are selling to the right legal company. Use the internet to find out as much as you can about your new customer before you open a new account.

If you don't use one of the credit reporting agencies, then check the references and use their experiences to help you to approve new customers. Bear in mind though that the customer will only give you his two or three best suppliers. He may be paying every other supplier well beyond terms. Without a third party report, you will have to take your chances.

A Comment On Providing Reference Checks:

I know that it sounds contradictory or selfish but I am not a big fan of requesting reference checks. Although most credit applications, including the one at the back of this guide include two or more suppliers' names, I would rather pay for a third party report since it will give me an unbiased view of how the customer pays his suppliers overall and not just the ones on the application.

I don't like giving credit references either unless I know the company I am giving the reference to. I won't give confidential information to a company I don't know. If you give references on your customer, make sure you have your customer's written permission to do so. Do it in writing and only if you include a clause that states you are providing the information in confidence and that the information will only be used to establish or approve credit. I recommend something like "The information provided is privileged and confidential. It is provided for the sole purpose of providing a credit reference and must not be disclosed to anyone other than the intended recipient."

If you can't give a favourable credit reference on your customer, you should decline the request rather than giving a bad reference. I've seen suppliers being sued because they gave out negative references or because the company that they gave the reference to did not keep the information confidential.

The reason I don't like asking for or giving reference checks is that anyone applying for credit will always use their best suppliers as references; those that they pay on time. I want to know about the ones they don't pay on time. I use the references on the credit application to help locate a customer who skips. If you know who else he was buying from, you have a better chance of finding him

The credit application in the appendix includes a clause that lets you recover legal or collection fees if you have to sue or place the account for collection. If you place an account for collection the agency will insist that you have this clause in your application or they will not try to collect the interest for you. Lawyers may or may not try to collect interest for you depending on the Courts.

The application also includes a personal guarantee. Surprisingly, a lot of customers sign the guarantee which is usually a foolish thing to do since that makes them both corporately and personally liable. If you get a personal guarantee you might have a better chance of collecting any disputed amounts if you point out that you have recourse against both the company and the guarantor. However, do not use the personal guarantee as the sole basis for approving credit. If there is no money in the business, the chances are that the guarantor has no money either. We'll talk in detail about personal guarantees later. For now, if you get a signature, good!

If the customer objects to one or more of the terms and conditions of your credit application, ask him to strike out the clause and initial it. Depending on what clause he disagrees with, you may want to accept his changes. For example, I wouldn't have a problem if an applicant strikes out the clause that says you can apply his payment the way you see fit. I might waive the retention of title clause if the customer is credit worthy. I wouldn't waive the terms of sale clause.

Third Party Reports
When opening a new account, you want answers to three questions;

- Who am I selling to?
- Will I get paid?
- When will I get paid?

To answer these questions, you can either rely on your credit application or buy a credit report. If you rely on your credit application, you are relying on the customer to provide you with the correct legal entity that will pay you. In most cases you can rely on the information provided. The three references he gives you will of course be the three suppliers that he pays on time. He won't tell you about any suppliers that he doesn't pay on time and he won't tell you if he has given any supplier an NSF cheque or if the supplier has had to place his account for collection.

If you're granting $5-10,000 or less you might be able to rely on this information to support your exposure as long as you keep the account current.

If you want to be as informed as possible, you should buy a credit report from one of the two primary Canadian reporting agencies, Dun & Bradstreet (D&B) www.dnb.ca or Equifax Canada www.Equifax.ca. Both provide valuable information and have been around long enough to outlast the competition. Both have also recognized that their market has changed. In the past, both D&B and Equifax required subscribers to purchase annual contracts with locked in pricing. If the subscriber didn't use the entire contract, the balance was forfeited. Both now allow pay as you go agreements. The cost per report is higher than purchasing a block of reports but I would suggest that unless you can accurately predict how many account you expect to open, that you go with the pay as you go option.

Let's look at the difference in the information provided by each;

Dun & Bradstreet (D&B)

D&B employs reporters to interview companies, solicit financial information and profile the principals' background and experience. D&B then adds the payment experience of its subscribers that provide their aging. D&B focuses on commercial credit and has an entire section dedicated to small business. You can download a sample report from the D&B website.

How to read a D&B report

Reading a D&B report can be overwhelming. Information about the size and scope of the business along with the background of the officers is very valuable. For most credit decisions you can probably rely on three key components;

Credit Score Class

This is a proprietary formula that D&B uses to predict severe delinquency over the next 12 months. D&B defines severe delinquency as 90 or more days past terms. The formula is based on trade experiences, past due accounts, negative payment comments, the control age of the business and financial information.

The score ranges from low risk (1) to high risk (5) with a moderate score being (3). A customer with a score of 5 presents a high risk of not paying you on time. A customer with a score of 1 will probably pay you on time.

5	4	3	2	1
High Risk		Moderate Risk		Low Risk

Financial Stress Class

This model predicts the likelihood of the business ceasing operations without paying all of its creditors or reorganizing over the next 12 months. It includes bankruptcy and proposals to creditors. The formula is based on payment experiences, past due accounts, the control age of the business, whether or not the business owns the facilities it operates in as well as financial information.

The score ranges from a low risk (1) to high risk of (5) with a moderate score of (3).

5	4	3	2	1
High Risk		Moderate Risk		Low Risk

D&B Paydex

D&B uses the payment experience of trade references to compile an index of how the business pays its suppliers. The index ranges from 100 for a business that pays its bills on time to 0 for a business that pays 120 days slow. The mid range score of 50 is roughly equal to 30 days slow.

D&B charts the Paydex trend over both a 3 month and a 12 month period. Often a business will slow payments to suppliers due to seasonal adjustments and this will show in the Paydex trends.

A Paydex score of 80 to 100 indicates a low risk of late payments. These customers will pay you on time or discount.

A Paydex score of 50-79 indicates a medium risk of late payments. These customers will pay you between 1 and 30 days beyond terms.

A Paydex score of less than 50 indicates a high risk of late payments. These customers will pay you 30 to 120 days beyond terms.

0	50	100
120 days slow	30 Days Slow	Pays On Time

Dun & Bradstreet introduced a risk management process about 25 years ago called Risk Assessment Manager (RAM) later replaced with DNBi which is an online program. I have implemented both RAM and DNBi and have found them to be valuable tools that let you build what D&B calls "scorecards" to help you manage your accounts. You can customize the scorecard or you can let D&B develop it for you. If you have the budget and IT staff to help implement the program, it may help you manage your credit operation. One of the primary advantages is that it lets staff make consistent decisions since your procedure and policy is built into the program.

Equifax Canada

Before we discuss how to read an Equifax report I need to provide you with a bit of background information since it reflects directly on the contents of the report. Prior to 1996 Creditel of Canada was the primary source of payment experience for Canadian companies. Creditel and its predecessor, Lumberman's Credit date back more than 100 years. Creditel was a member owned group of credit managers who met monthly to exchange information on mutual accounts. We met by industry group under a confidentiality agreement. Creditel compiled the data from those meetings but did not maintain an adequate cross referencing system. As a result, information was often disjointed and not comprehensive enough to base a decision on. When Equifax bought Creditel it embarked on a comprehensive project to integrate the data under the same business name and the current reports are much more reliable. However please make sure that you have the right customer.

How to read an Equifax report

Equifax still relies heavily on its subscribers to provide the information contained in its reports. Credit managers still belong to industry groups that meet monthly. Those meetings are now run by Equifax. The payment experience from contributing members is consolidated and used to provide two scores.

Credit Information Score (CIS)

This component of the report is based on a number of factors;

- how long the subject has been on file with Equifax
- how promptly the subject pays its suppliers
- the number of references on file
- payment trends
- number of derogatory items on file (writs, suits, judgments and collections)
- date of the most recent derogatory item
- derogatory items as a percentage of total dollars owed

The CIS ranges from a low of 0 to a high of 70 with a score of 30 or more indicating a high risk

```
0_____30_____70
Low Risk          High Risk          Very High Risk
```

How you use the score depends on your procedure and policy but I recommend that if the score is 30 or higher that you ask for security or limit your exposure. If the score is 40 or higher, ask for cash.

Payment Index

Based on the payment experience of the suppliers reporting to Equifax, a payment index is provided on a scale of 0 to 100 with 0 being a prompt payer and 100 being the worst payer. The payment index is similar to the number of days late so an index of 40 indicates that the subject pays its suppliers on average 40 days beyond the due date.

This index can be significantly influenced by the number of suppliers who report their payment experience. Not all suppliers report and not even all members of the various industry groups report. If there are less than 3 payment experiences listed, I would not put much weight on this index. I have seen reports that list only one supplier even though there were many suppliers selling to the subject. The one supplier reported very slow payments so the subject had a very poor payment index even though most suppliers were not reporting. Equifax reports the number of suppliers in both the CIS and the payment trend section.

```
0_____30_____100
Pays            Pays            Probably
On Time         30 Days         Out Of
                Late            Business
```

Equifax provides trends for both the CIS and the Paydex and may provide graphs to help you to spot those trends. Equifax also provides records of NSF cheques, collection claims, legal suits, judgments and bankruptcies. The report may also include a bank reference along with some history on the business.

Equifax has recently developed a risk scoring process that may prove to be valuable. However, I find myself at odds with some of the scoring components. I'll wait and see what the track record looks like in a year or two.

If your budget has room, I would encourage you to buy both reports on customers that you grant larger credit limits to. If you have to make a choice, I would recommend D&B as the better of the two reporting agencies since it includes information about the key management of the company.

If you're looking for a risk management system, you may want to look at Onsite's program called Strategically Targeted Accounts Receivable (STAR) that allows you to rate your customers according to risk not only overall but within your own portfolio. STAR then allows you to allocate resources based on the risk associated with the customers. STAR includes scores from both D&B and Equifax.

Addendum:

As at the time of writing this guide, I've just been made aware of a new credit reporting agency, B2B Credit Chex. www.b2bcreditchex.com B2B is relatively new to the Canadian market and I haven't yet used them so I can't express an opinion.

B2B says they conduct a fresh investigation for each report and store your credit files electronically for you. They say that you can customize your application and they will store it online for you. Like D&B and Equifax they have a pay as you go option and they claim that all of their reports are credit insurance approved. If that claim is accurate, they could be an excellent source of information.

I will investigate further and if you send me an email at ian@onsitecreditgroup.com I'll let you know what I find out.

Banks and Bank References

As you probably know from your own experience, banks don't like to take risks when loaning money. The bank wants a guarantee that it will get its money back plus interest and will usually demand that all of the assets of the business be used to secure the loan along with the personal guarantee of the owner(s).

The most common security banks use is a General Security Agreement (GSA) which pledges all of the company's assets to the bank. This includes inventory, accounts receivable and equipment. If the asset has value the bank wants it. Banks won't lend up to the full value of either the inventory or the accounts receivable but will discount both to make sure it does not over extend the line of credit.

Most credit applications including the one in the appendix provide for the name and address of the applicant's bank. I no longer have use for bank references and would discount any information that the bank provides. I use this information to find the customer if he leaves town without paying me.

You need to understand that the banker has a vested interest in getting suppliers to provide product to his client. The more inventory that there is, the more secure the bank's loan is. Banks will almost never tell you about returned cheques or if the loan is in default. If you get a favourable bank reference you are more likely to ship on open terms. Bankers won't admit this but I can assure you from personal experience that it's true.

I recall having an NSF cheque in my hand while talking to the customer's banker who assured me that his client had never issued a returned cheque. I've also received a favourable bank reference while a trustee in bankruptcy was locking the doors to the business.

In the case of a loan default the bank can seize all of the assets of the business and doesn't have to explain its actions to anyone. The most common way banks do this is to appoint a receiver. The receiver takes over the business and liquidates the assets for the benefit of the bank which pays his fees. In a receivership, there is no requirement for the receiver to tell the trade creditors anything about what he is doing on behalf of the bank. The only way to force disclosure is for the suppliers to petition the debtor into bankruptcy.

If you have sold product to a business that is in receivership you can demand the return of any product that you shipped within the last 30 days as long as you can identify the goods and prove that you have not been paid. I cover 30 day goods in depth later. If you have an Inventory Security Agreement (covered later in this guide) then you can usually get your product back even if more than 30 days have gone by.

Treat any information you obtain from a bank carefully and understand the bank's position.

If you decide to request bank reports, or if the third party report contains one, here's how to interpret them;

Current account opened: will tell you how long the business has been dealing with the bank.

Current account balance: will tell you how much money the company has in its chequing account. This is usually stated as a range rather than an actual amount. A low 5 figure balance means $30-50,000 ($XX,XXX is five figures). Count the figures from right to left ignoring any commas or dollar signs.

Returned cheques: generally the comment will cover the past 3 months (don't expect full disclosure)

Loan Date: the date that the loan was taken out

Loan Amount: this is usually the maximum amount the bank will loan and may be stated as the actual amount or may also be stated as a range. Low 6 figures means $100-400,000 ($XXX,XXX is six figures). Mid 6 figures means $500,000-$700,000 and high 6 figures means between $700,000 and $999,999. Seven figures means $1 million or more.

Balance Outstanding or Balance owing: will also be stated as a range

Security: this is the security that the bank holds and will usually include a GSA, all book debts (accounts receivable) and a first floating charge over all of the assets of the company. Personal guarantees are also usual although they may not be listed on the report

Although your credit application may include your customer's approval to conduct a bank reference the bank may not want to provide one to you unless your customer contacts the bank directly and instructs the bank to provide the reference.

I have seen suppliers who use the bank line of credit to set the customer's credit limit. This is very risky since the bank is secured and your probably aren't.

Going it Alone

As I mentioned earlier, a lot of business owners sell based on relationships. They start out selling to customers that they know; someone they went to school with, a neighbour or the first customer that gave them an order for their product or service. Relationships are important but in difficult times or in case of a dispute friendships can quickly disappear.

Some of my clients have gotten themselves into serious difficulty by selling based on knowing the customer but not doing proper due diligence either when the account was first opened or as the business (and the risk) increased.

If you decide that you can't afford a credit or bank report and you're feeling lucky*, you can still grant open terms as long as you understand the risk. If you want to waive credit checks, here is a guideline for you to use based on the length of time your customer has been in business;

Conservative Approach	Moderate Approach	Aggressive Approach
1 Year or less, CASH	1 Year or less, CASH	1 Year or less, CASH
2-3 years, $1-$3,000	2-3 years, $3-$5,000	2-3 years, up to $5,000
3 plus years up to $5,000	3 plus years up to $7,500	3 plus years up to $10,000

Set the credit limit based on the average 30 day purchases of the customer plus 50% to allow 15 days for the mailing of invoices and the receipt of payment. For example if your customer buys $2,000 every 30 days set the credit limit at $3,000.

Using this process you will build in an early warning system. If the customer exceeds the credit limit, one of two things is happening;

- the customer is buying more than expected when the limit was set. If the account is current, you can increase the credit limit up to the above guidelines.
- the customer is paying you slower than 45 days in which case you want to find out why before deciding to change the credit limit. Don't keep adjusting the limit just to keep the account from going over limit or you will lose control very quickly

*If you're feeling lucky maybe you should put your money on one turn of the roulette wheel in Vegas. I guarantee your odds of winning are better than granting open credit terms without proper credit checks.

Personal Guarantees

I have *never* taken a personal guarantee in lieu of equity in the business. If the owner does not believe in his business enough to put his money at risk, then I'm not going to put mine at risk.

The owner might live in a mansion and drive an expensive car but both could be rented. You can search title to the property and the car but even if he owns both you have no way of knowing who else he has given a personal guarantee to. For sure he's given it to the bank and the banker will know he's in trouble long before you do.

You can sue on a personal guarantee but it's expensive and you have no way of predicting the outcome. I look at personal guarantees like playing poker. If I have real money on the table but the customer is using Monopoly money, he has nothing to lose but I can't win. I want the owner to have at least as much at risk as I do. I call it "having skin in the game." If the business owner has no skin in the game, I'm not going to put my money at risk. When we look at financial statements I'll show you how to determine how much the business owner has at risk and how you can still grant credit if there is little or none

You'll notice that I include a personal guarantee in my credit application. If the customer signs it, I won't complain and it may help get my money back but I don't use it to set the credit limit. If the customer starts to dispute the balance he owes me then I'll send him a copy of the application and remind him that he's both corporately and personally liable.

Types of Business in Canada

In Canada there are 3 main types of businesses; sole proprietorships, partnerships and corporations. You need to understand the relative risk of selling to each.

A. A sole proprietorship is a business that is owned and managed by one person. The owner of the business is liable for all of the debt of the business. His personal assets are not separate from the business. If the business fails his creditors can sue the business owner personally. This is the easiest and least expensive business to set up in Canada. If you are selling to a sole proprietorship you are in fact selling to the owner personally. Any income that the business earns is taxed at the owner's personal tax rate. It is not common for business owners to leave their personal assets at risk.

B. In a partnership, each partner is liable for the debts of the other partner, even if the second partner was unaware of the debt. There can be as few as two partners or an unlimited number of partners. Credit managers tend to avoid selling to partnerships since they tend to be difficult to control. If the partners have internal disagreements, it can be hard to get your money back without litigation. In credit, we have a saying "a partnership is a sinking ship." The are also Limited Liability partnerships which are usually either law firms or accounting firms. Each partner is only liable up to the amount he or she has invested in the business. Again, the relationship of the partners can make it difficult to collect.

C. Corporations are the most common form of businesses in Canada since the owner's personal assets are not at risk. The company is treated in law as if it were a third person. A corporation can sue and be sued but the liability is limited to the paid in capital and the retained earnings of the business. You cannot sue the owners of the business for the debt of the company unless you have a personal guarantee. Corporations will have "Limited, LTD, Inc., Corporation or Corp." contained in the name.

Welcome Letters

Send a welcome letter to every new customer (see sample in the appendix) to advise him of your terms, the credit limit and who he should contact if he has any issues. If the customer later says that his terms are different than yours, you can send him a copy of the both the credit application and the welcome letter to show him that your terms are the ones that count.

Minimizing Your Risk

Unless you have an absolute monopoly on your products or service you probably have to provide your customers with credit terms in order to be competitive but there are ways to minimize your risk;

1. Get Paid First: Before Everyone Else, Including The Bank (even in a bankruptcy)

Trade creditors, those who supply product or services* to customers on credit terms are usually the last ones to be paid. In the case of a bankruptcy, insolvency or a proposal you may never get paid at all. The reason for this is that a secured lender (usually a bank) uses your product as security for a loan even when the product hasn't been paid for. The bank is allowed to do this through a security agreement with the customer that lets the bank seize any inventory even when the supplier has not been paid. The bank can then sell the inventory for any price it wants and has no legal obligation to the supplier who provided the product in the first place.

The bank only loans a percentage of the value of the inventory so that when it seizes your product it can hold a fire sale, collect part of its loan and reduce its losses. To be fair, there are a lot of businesses that would not qualify for financing if the bank wasn't allowed to take the inventory as collateral. However, it doesn't have to be *your* inventory that the customer uses as security. You can register a security agreement that forces the bank to pay you in full or allow you to take your inventory back before it seizes the rest of the inventory and holds that fire sale.

* Unfortunately you can't use the PPSA to secure services, only tangible items.

Here's how it works;

As part of your credit granting process you can negotiate an Inventory Security Agreement (ISA) combined with a Purchase Money Security Interest (PMSI) that states that in the event of a loan default, a bankruptcy or proposal you are entitled to be paid first or allowed to take back your inventory *before anyone else gets paid, including the bank.*

Once you have the agreement in place, it must be registered within the province that the business is being conducted in. (So, if your customer is in British Columbia you must register there even if you are in Ontario). This is referred to as the Personal Property Security Act (PPSA) and all common law provinces have such an act in place. Your security even follows your product into your customer's accounts receivable so that you have the right to recover the money from the end user even if your inventory has been sold. If your customer defaults on a loan, you now have the legal right to demand payment before everyone else, including the bank. If the customer files for bankruptcy the Trustee has a legal obligation to make sure you are paid first.

Negotiating and registering a security agreement used to require a lawyer and hundreds of dollars in fees. Now, your agreement can be filed for less than $50.00 for a period of up to 7 years. I use a company called Canadian Securities Registration Systems, Ltd. (www.csrs.ca) and I strongly recommend that you use a third party to register your agreement since any simple filing error will make your agreement unenforceable.

Although I've included a template ISA in the appendix, I suggest that you ask your lawyer for an opinion before you adopt it within your company.

Pitfalls to watch for;

Even with an ISA in place, you may not get paid if your customer decides to have an inventory sale without telling you. If you think that your customer is liquidating your product, you have the right to demand that he return it to you under the terms of the security agreement. You also need to be able to identify your product, usually by serial number. Include the serial numbers on your invoice as an extra step.

If a Trustee seizes your product, contact him immediately and demand payment or the return of the inventory even if you aren't able to identify it fully. I'd rather be aggressive than passive when involved in a bankruptcy. The Trustee will want to take the easy way to collect his money and will not want to be involved in litigation.

If you get an ISA from a customer, make sure you store the original in a safe place. You can't use a copy to enforce your security.

You may also want to conduct periodic inventory checks especially if the customer seems to be stocking up. I had a customer who kept ordering product while according to the unpaid invoices he should have had 2-3 months worth of my product on hand. When I visited him to conduct an inventory check I found that my product was stacked 5 boxes high. The first 2 boxes were full but the top 3 were empty because he had sold the product and not paid me. By stacking the boxes he assumed that I would not climb up and look into the top 3. I did eventually get paid but put the account on cash with order.

2. Use Credit Insurance* Instead of Open Terms

Credit insurance can be incredibly complicated and I can't cover all of the aspects here but I can provide you with an overview which may help you to decide if you want to explore the option further.

As the insurers point out, accounts receivable are likely one of your largest financial assets. You have insurance on your warehouse and inventory and likely have insurance on your key employees, but few small businesses have insurance on their accounts receivable.

Credit insurance is like buying car insurance for your accounts receivable. Instead of insuring your car in case of an accident, you're insuring your accounts receivable in case the customer doesn't pay you. Just like car insurance, you pay an annual premium which is based on your predicted sales. If you don't have an accident (or all of your customers pay you) then the insurance company keeps your premium. The rate you pay will vary based on a number of factors but it will generally cost about 0.50% of your annual sales.

There are 2 primary types of policies; key debtor and whole turnover cover. The Key debtor covers only your largest (likely most credit worthy) customers and the whole turnover cover is for all of your customers. You cannot "cherry pick" the accounts you want to cover because the insurance company makes its money by charging you for *every* account not just the high risk accounts. They won't just take your problem accounts off your hands.

The insurance company will set the limit that you can sell to each customer and if you exceed that limit the coverage is limited to the amount they approved. Any amount over that is 100% your risk. The insurer will also set the maximum amount that you or your staff can approve without getting their approval first. This is called a discretionary limit and it's based on the level and qualifications of the person who manages your credit on a day to day basis.

On a day to day basis you ship orders up to the approved credit limit for each account. You still have to collect the accounts and you can only request insurance coverage once you have exhausted your collection efforts or the customer goes out of business.

In addition to the premiums, there are other costs as well;

(a) The insurance company will set a non-qualifying loss which is like the deductible on your car except that you can't get a credit insurance policy without a deductible. Typically the first $1,000.00 of any loss is 100% your risk. The insurer simply deducts it from the balance like it never existed.
(b) Then there is an aggregate first loss which is like saying "we don't cover you for your first accident"
(c) The datum line is an amount below which the account is not covered (i.e. your small accounts)
(d) The minimum retention is the minimum amount of each loss that you have to pay for yourself
(e) Co-Insurance is a percentage of each loss that is not covered by the policy
(f) The maximum liability is the maximum that the insurance company is liable to pay on all losses during a policy period

So, you might think that credit insurance will keep you from having any bad debts but the reality is that you are still at risk. The insurance agent will point out that you will be able to increase sales to customers that you would not have considered selling to before, that you won't have to set a bad debt reserve and that your bank will be ready to lend you more money against insured receivables. While there is some truth to those claims, I have never found that credit insurance was cost justified. I would rather put my money into proper due diligence and hire someone capable of making those kinds of decisions.

If you decide to apply for credit insurance, be prepared to provide full disclosure including;

- full financial statements for the last 3 or more years
- total number of active accounts,

- total credit sales
- days sales outstanding
- bad debt write offs
- do you have a formal credit policy?
- who manages the credit process?
- how do you establish credit limits?
- at what credit limit are financial statements required?
  (if any of this sounds familiar please see "first things first" in this guide)

*(Credit Insurance is generally only available to companies with annual sales in excess of $1 million. Insurers are not interested in quoting below that amount)

3. Factor (Discount) Your Receivables

Factoring is selling your accounts receivable to a third party (called a factor) at a discount in exchange for immediate payment. Factoring is different than using your accounts receivable as security for a bank loan. Factoring is not a loan; it is the sale of a financial asset. A bank loan involves only you and your bank while factoring involves you, the factor and your customer. In the case of a bank loan, the bank is basing the loan on the credit worthiness of your company while the factor is basing the funding on the value of the accounts receivable. Once you sell your receivables, they will no longer show on your balance sheet (but all that cash will).

A bank will discount the value of your receivables since it has no way of determining the value of the balances your customers owe you. Generally banks won't loan against any past due invoices. If you have followed my guidelines in developing a proper procedure and policy the bank will probably loan you a higher amount against the receivables but banks <u>always</u> discount the value of your A/R.

Factoring can be useful if you need to free up the money in your receivables, if you need working capital quickly or if you don't want the responsibility of collecting your own receivables. If the customer is past due, the factor's staff make the collection calls.

A factor will spend time reviewing your financial statements, your receivables and your credit granting process (which is sound because you've been using this guide) in order to determine the level of financing that you qualify for. Once approved, you sell your invoices to the factor at a discount and the factor now owns the receivable.

The factor will instruct you to have all of your customers' change where they remit payment to. The customer no longer sends the payment to you. Instead payment goes to a lockbox which is a bank account that is managed by the factor. Your customers will be notified that you are using a factor. This can be a roadblock for some small business owners since they don't want the customer to know that their invoice has been sold to a third party but objections can be overcome with the help of the factor.

Once the factor has your invoice, you will be financed 85-90% of the value within 24 hours. The balance of the invoice, less fees will be paid to you once the invoice is paid by your customer. The factor is responsible for collecting your accounts receivable for you so you don't need a collection staff. However if the customer doesn't pay the factor, you will be responsible which is why you follow this guide in granting credit.

Unlike Credit Insurance, factoring is available to businesses with much smaller annual sales. Generally a company that does about $100-200,000 in business will qualify for factoring. I am a broker for one of the largest factors in Canada and would be pleased to discuss the option further if you email me at ian@onsitecreditgroup.com

The costs of factoring vary from case to case but the approximate cost is 1.5% to 2.0% of the invoice value. If you trade off a cash discount in exchange for immediate payment and someone else collecting the A/R for you, it can be beneficial. In the index I have used a simplified example to show the benefits of factoring.

4. If You Export Product, Use the Export Development Corporation

The Export Development Corporation (EDC) is a Crown corporation that insures goods and services that Canadian businesses export to other countries. The EDC will insure your receivables up to 90% of the value of your invoice with rates varying based on risk. There are eligibility requirements that can be found at www.edc.ca

5. Arrange For Bank or Corporate Guarantees

I once had a customer that I would not grant open terms to because he had been both corporately and personally bankrupt previously yet he moved more than $1 million of my product so I had to find a way to sell him. The solution was to require an irrevocable* letter of credit from his bank.

A Stand By Letter of Credit essentially transfers the responsibility for payment from your customer to his banker. The banker guarantees that you will be paid as long as you meet the terms and conditions in the letter which usually is to deliver the goods or services requested by the customer. You provide the customer with open credit terms up to the value of the letter of credit and as long as he pays you, the letter of credit will not be drawn upon. It's your responsibility to collect from the customer until he either can't or won't pay you in which case you present the letter of credit to his bank and demand payment. The bank will either have the customer pay you or the bank is obliged to make the payment.

The bank will require the customer to post some kind of security (usually in the form of cash or negotiable bonds) equal to the value of the letter of credit. That way, if the bank has to pay the supplier it simply takes the money out of the customer's account. If there is no money in the customer's bank account, it's not your problem but the bank's. If your customer does not pay you then you make a demand to the bank for payment supported by all of the documentation required by the bank. This will usually consist of a copy of the customer's purchase order, the invoices that are not paid and proof of delivery.

The letter of credit will usually be for a specific time period so you need to make sure that you either renew it before it expires or make some other arrangement to ship product to the customer. I have required letters of credit from new customers for a period of a year or two until they can establish a prompt payment pattern and then I have released the letter of credit.

Letters of credit deal in documents not goods. Please make sure that you store the original letter of credit from the bank in a safe place. You cannot sue based on a photocopy. Your banker may be able to help you negotiate the letter and may be able to store the original for you.

My customer tried to revoke his letter of credit every six months or so but I would not allow him to unless his bank transferred funds to my bank to pay 100% of his outstanding account.

Be careful that you keep the account within the limit of the letter of credit. If you ship more than the limit, the rest is at your risk, not the bank's.

*An irrevocable letter of credit can't be revoked or amended unless you agree. A revocable letter of credit can be revoked or amended by the customer's bank for any reason without notification. Don't bother with a letter of credit unless it's irrevocable.

If you're selling to a subsidiary of a much larger organization and you're not comfortable selling to the subsidiary then you can ask the parent company to provide you with a corporate guarantee. It may be insulting to your customer but sometimes a child needs its parent to help him learn to walk before starting to run. Be careful however since it can happen the other way around as well. Blockbuster Inc., the U.S. parent of Blockbuster Canada Co used the assets of the Canadian subsidiary to guarantee its debt. When the parent filed for bankruptcy the movie studios forced the Canadian subsidiary into receivership even though the Canadian operations were supposedly profitable.

Setting Credit Limits Over $25,000

I've always made it a policy to ask for financial statements from any customer that wants a credit limit over $25,000. Depending on your tolerance for risk you might set the maximum lower. If you'll notice on the sample credit application, it states that financial statements might be necessary to support the credit request. Don't include a specific amount in case your policy changes. You don't want to have to reprint your credit application if the amount changes. If the customer declines your request, you can still give him a credit limit up to $25,000 once you have completed your credit investigation.

I do not recommend granting any customer unsecured credit in excess of $25,000 without reviewing financial statements. Your customer could not borrow $25,000 from his banker without providing both financial statements and security. The bank will then want to see updated financials every quarter or at least every six months.

A financial statement review will answer 3 key questions;

- will I be paid?
- will I be paid on time?
- how much risk am I taking?

In this section I'll show you how to answer all three questions with a simplified financial review of a sample financial statement.

Simplified Financial Analysis

Every financial statement, audited or not includes a balance sheet similar to the one below;

Part A of the balance sheet

Current Assets		Current Liabilities	
Cash	$10,000	Bank Loan	$60,000
Accounts Receivable	$35,000	Accounts Payable	$23,000
Inventory	$50,000	Income Taxes	$3,000
Other Current Assets	$3,000	Customer Deposits	$5,000
Total Current Assets	$98,000	Total Current Liabilities	$91,000

The working capital of a company is the total current assets less the total current liabilities. In this case, the company has a working capital of $7,000 ($98,000-$91,000). Most of that working capital can be converted into cash relatively quickly so the customer should be able to meet its payables on time. Credit managers like to see a current ratio (current assets / current liabilities) of 1:1 or more.

This customer has a current ratio of ($98,000 / $91,000) 1.08. In this case, the customer can sell inventory and collect accounts receivable quickly in order to pay its suppliers, including you.

If the customer has a current ratio of less than 1:1 you can anticipate that you will be paid beyond your terms since the customer needs to sell his inventory and collect his accounts receivable before he can pay you.

Part B of the balance sheet

Fixed Assets		Long Term Liabilities	
Equipment and Furniture	$100,000	Long Term Debt	$25,000
		Paid in Capital	$50,000
		Retained Earnings	$32,000
Total Assets	$198,000	Total Liabilities	$198,000

In the sample above, the owner has invested $50,000 of his own money, the business has made profits of $32,000 and the owner has kept those profits in the business in the form of retained earnings. So, the owner has $82,000 at risk.

The bank will have a first charge against all of the assets of the company to secure its line of credit. In the case of a loan default, the bank will seize assets in the following order;

Cash	$10,000	which is 100% recoverable	$10,000
Inventory	$50,000	which it will discount by	~25% $37,500
Accounts Receivable	$35,000	which it will discount by	~25% $26,250
Other Current Assets	$3,0000	which it will discount by	%100 $0
Total	$98,000	Total estimated recovery	$73,750

In this sample the bank would be able to recover its full loan balance quickly while leaving what's left of the business to the owners and unsecured creditors.

This sample customer would appear to be a low risk for a supplier granting an unsecured credit limit of around $25,000. Of course your tolerance for risk might be lower or higher but this analysis should give you a good idea of a simplified financial statement.

To find out where the company is going, follow the money;

- are the owners reinvesting the profits into the company to grow it for the future?
- are the owners buying new equipment, computers, software etc to make the company more efficient?
- are profits being used to pay down debt so that the balance sheet improves?
OR
- are the owners paying themselves large bonuses even if the company doesn't make a profit?
- are the owners taking their original investment back out so that they don't have as much at risk?
- are the owners making poor management decisions that put the company (and you) at risk?

Self Prepared Financial Statements

Never grant credit based on financial statements that the customer has prepared himself without a review by an accountant. This includes Excel spreadsheets and software packages like QuickBooks, AccPacc and Simply Accounting. As I tell my clients, give me a spreadsheet and I'll show you that I'm a millionaire; just don't ask me to prove it.

Different types of independently prepared financial statements

Compiled; the accountant gets information from the management of the company and puts it into the proper financial form. The accountant makes himself familiar with the industry but does not express an opinion on the accuracy of the information provided by the management. The management is responsible for the accuracy of the data provided to the accountant.

Reviewed; the accountant reviews the information he is given by management and makes himself familiar with the industry. Management is still responsible for the data but the accountant asks more questions about the information provided to make sure that it seems accurate. The accountant issues a report that provides limited assurances to anyone who reads the report (usually the owners and the bank). The accountant will make a note that the statements are correct as far as he knows but he does not express an opinion

Audited; the accountant tests the internal controls to make sure that no errors or fraud takes place. He confirms the data he is given with third parties like banks, customers and suppliers. He observes physical inventory counts and talks to employees.

The accountant expresses his opinion that the financials meet the standards set by the accounting profession.* The accountant issues a report highlighting any issues that he has concerns about. The accountant will usually make comments about the nature of the business and the market in general. If there are any significant items, he will report them in his findings. All publicly traded companies are audited. (* the accountant may qualify his comments)

The accountant, whether he audits the statement or not has a responsibility to comment on any items that he might find unusual. These comments are made at the end of the statement in the notes that accompany the review or audit. Because he is governed by the accounting principles and subject to the rules of accounting he has a moral and a legal obligation to comment on any items that he is not sure of or if he disagrees with management. Often the notes to the statement will tell you more about the financials than the numbers themselves. The two items most frequently commented on are revenue (sales) and goodwill. Be sure to read the notes and ask questions if you are unclear about any comments the accountant makes.

Alternate Sources of Financial Information

If your policy is to require financial statements to support an increased credit limit, you may find that your customer won't provide financials especially if it is a private company. That does not mean that you can't find a way to support the increase nor does it mean that you have to increase your risk.

Every company no matter how private has either an accountant or a bank manager either of which can give you enough information to assess the risk. Ask your customer to have the accountant or the bank manager provide you with a comment on both the working capital and the equity of the business. Getting a general comment will allow you to determine if you will be paid and when you will be paid without violating the customer's confidentiality.

Let me explain further;

- the banker or accountant will give you a range similar to low 5 figures, mid 6 figures etc. for both the working capital and the equity
- using those ranges you can determine the risk involved (see the section on Banks and Bank References for a full explanation)

If the bank or accountant won't give you ranges, ask him if the working capital is positive (meaning the customer can pay you on time) and if there is equity in the company (meaning the owner has his own money at risk). If the bank or accountant won't give you any information then I suggest that you politely decline the customer's request for an increased credit limit. You can't afford to put yourself at risk.

Selling Service on Credit

At Onsite all we sell is service. We don't make anything and we can't take our services back if our customer doesn't pay. For that reason we insist on partial payment (usually 50%) when we sign an agreement with the client and progress payments as the project meets various milestones. We usually ask for another 25% when the project is essentially complete and the balance on completion.

Do we run into objections? Yes, but we won't start a project until our client has invested in its outcome. It's too easy for a client to change his mind, for budget approval to be withdrawn or the sponsor to leave the company. We also can't force the customer to adapt any of our recommendations so the client may not see the benefits of the project and withhold payment.

If you're selling a service I suggest that you cover at least your costs before starting a project, that you get a written agreement and that if any payment is missed that you defer further work until you are paid.

Comprehensive Financial Analysis

Except in the case of fraud, it is usually possible to predict the future of a company by analyzing the past financial statements over a period of several years. Unless there has been a change in ownership, the company is not likely to do things differently in future. The key ratios will show an analyst the direction the company is going in based on past experience. By comparing the key ratios to standard industry ratios, the analyst can gain an insight into how the company is doing relative to its industry peers. Financial analysis is a skill that has to be developed over several years' experience combined with formal training. "Don't try this at home"

In the appendix I have included a sample of the kind of extensive analysis that Onsite performs for our clients. We provide all of the key ratios as well as a prediction on whether the company will still be in business in 12-18 months. We're so sure of our prediction that if we're wrong, you don't pay us. The sample in the index is a publicly traded Canadian company that was highly leveraged. Their auditors made them restate goodwill (an intangible asset) to the point that the company became insolvent and was at risk of self liquidating.

In the appendix I highlight some of the key areas of concern that we uncovered in our analysis and warned our client about. The company eventually restructured which included a change in ownership. Onsite can do similar analysis on your customers if you are not comfortable determining the risk. In fact, our analysis is so good that if we get it wrong, you don't pay.

Goodwill

As you probably know from your own financial statement, goodwill can make up a large part of the customers balance sheet. Credit managers instantly dismiss goodwill, giving it no value whatsoever. Why? Because goodwill only has value if the business is sold as a going concern and then only as much as the new buyer will pay for it.

If the business fails, goodwill has no value since only the tangible assets will be saleable

Accountants are becoming much more aggressive about writing down intangible assets like goodwill because of the current economic climate. Based on the large frauds in the U.S. the accounting standards are becoming more stringent.

If you see goodwill or other intangibles on the customer's balance sheet, give them no value at all.

Cash Is King

In the end, the only way you're sure not to have any bad debt losses is to sell for cash. As I said at the beginning of this section, unless you have a monopoly on your goods or service, you probably have to provide some kind of terms. But if you can't manage the risk or if your customers aren't credit worthy, you can ask for cash before you sell your product or service. There are no laws, commercial or otherwise that says you have to grant credit terms.

SECTION 3

Receivable Management

Collecting Accounts Receivable

I started my credit career as a repo guy for one of the Big 3 auto makers so I learned my street smarts before I got my book smarts. I know that collecting is not for everyone and that a lot of people avoid it if possible, especially business owners who have conflicted goals. You often know the customer personally and may feel awkward asking for money even though you have provided the goods and services. It's usually best if you delegate routine collections to your staff and act as mediator if problems come up. If you completed your procedure and policy earlier in the guide, your staff has a blueprint to work from and you can resolve any disputes.

Regardless of what products or services you provide, your customers fall into one of three categories;

1. Those that can and will pay you on more or less on time.
2. Those that will eventually pay you; just not right now.
3. Those that can't or won't pay you.

How you collect from each is different;
1. For the customers that pays you on time;
    -   mail invoices at least twice per week
    -   send a statement at the beginning of each month
    -   check the aging mid month to look for any short payment or missed invoices
    -   resolve any disputes quickly
    -   keep sales informed, identify for growth

2. For the customers that usually pay you late;
    -   call after delivery to make sure everything was delivered as ordered with no shortages or damages
    -   send invoices promptly, don't save up invoices to save on postage
    -   send a statement at the beginning of each month
    -   make the first collection call one week before the due date of the invoice to identify any problems
    -   keep sales involved

3. For the customers that can't or won't pay you;
    -   make sure the customer can't get more product or service from you on credit
    -   find out exactly what the problem is as soon as possible
    -   don't hide the problem from others in the company who need to know and may be able to help
    -   don't put off bringing in expert help

A Typical Collection Call

Let's look at a typical collection call and how most untrained collection staff would react. Here's the situation; it's just before month end and sales has brought me a new order from Fred for $2500.00. Fred needs the product tomorrow and sales want me to approve the shipment. Fred's account looks like this;

Fred's Company Inc.
Credit Limit; $6000

Total	Current	1-30	31-60	61-90	90+
$5500	$0	$500	$2500	$2500	$0

New Order Pending for $2500

I call Fred because shipping the new order will put him over his credit limit. The conversation might go something like;

Me: "Hey Fred, its Ian calling from Onsite . . ."

Fred: "Hey Ian, glad you called. Just put your cheque in the mail. You're not going to delay my order are you?"

Me: "Of course not Fred, I just had to call to make sure your cheque is on the way since the new order would put you over your limit."

Fred: "Why should that be a problem, just increase my limit, I've never stiffed you before and I'm not going to now. Just raise the limit."

Me: "OK, I'll take a look at your account and get back to you. Thanks for sending the cheque."

I ship the order and two days later I get the cheque but it's only for $750.00. Now Fred's account looks like this;

Fred's Company Inc.
Credit Limit; $6000

Total	Current	1-30	31-60	61-90	90+
$7250	$2500	$500	$2500	$1750	$0

So, I call Fred back;

Me: "Hey Fred, its Ian from Onsite . . ."

Fred: "Hey Ian did you increase my credit limit yet?"

Me: "I can't Fred. You're account is still past due and now you're way over your limit. You told me you were sending me a cheque."

Fred: "And I did."

Me: "But it's only for $750.00 and I needed $2500."

Fred: "You didn't say that and you didn't ask me how much my cheque was for. If you had told me you needed more, I would have paid it."

Me: "Well I shipped the order based on my understanding that you were sending me at least as much so that you would be within your credit limit."

Fred: "No problem, just increase my limit."

Me: "Sorry, policy won't allow me to unless you can send be the balance over 90 days and then I can do a review."

Fred: "Sorry, I can't. My customer hasn't paid me so you'll have to wait."

This is how a typical untrained collector might handle the call. I probably won't hear from Fred again until he needs another order. Meanwhile I'll go through the whole month hoping Fred stays in business long enough to pay his account.

Getting Specific

I train my staff and clients that collecting is about specifics;
Get a specific commitment for;

- a specific amount
- from a specific person
- on a specific day
- sent by a specific method

Then follow up to make sure the commitment is kept.
With that in mind, let's go back;
Here's how the call should have gone;

Me: "Hey Fred, its Ian calling from Onsite . . ."
Fred: "Hey Ian, glad you called. Just put your cheque in the mail. You're not going to delay my order are you?"
Me: "I hope not Fred. How much was the cheque for?"
Fred: "$750.00 for the oldest invoice."
Me: "Ouch, that's going to cause me a problem."
Fred: "No problem, just increase my limit and ship the order."
Me: "Sorry Fred, policy is that we need to bring your account current before I can consider an increase. At the rate your buying from us your credit limit looks to be right. Can you pay me the $1,750 that's still 61-90 days so that we can get your new order out to you?"
Fred: "OK, if it means you'll ship my order to-day I'll get you a cheque next week."
Me: "I wish I could agree to that Fred but I need to bring your account down so that I can keep you within your limit. I'm going to give you my bank information so that you can wire the money to me and then we can get your order out to you."
Fred: "I guess I have to since I need that order to-day."

I wait until Fred wires the money before I release the new order then two days later I get the $750.00 cheque so now Fred's account looks like this;

Fred's Company Inc.
Credit Limit; $6000

Total	Current	1-30	31-60	61-90	90+
$5500	$2500	$500	$2500	$0	$0

Going back to specifics, Fred gave me a specific commitment for a specific amount ($1,750) to be wire transferred into my bank to-day so that I could ship his order. I waited until I confirmed the transfer before releasing the order. If the transfer did not happen I would have called Fred back and asked him why he didn't keep the commitment he made to me.

It's important to understand that one of the reasons to keep an account current is to keep the customer in a ready to buy position. If I let Fred owe me $7250 then I can't ship him new orders. He may then take his business elsewhere which means I lose the sale and I don't have any leverage to help me collect the past due balance.

Making Collection Calls

Many people aren't comfortable making collection calls so they let the customer off the hook by accepting a vague promise of a payment. You must get a specific commitment or the customer may take advantage of you. Remember that it's the customer that is not keeping his side of the bargain. You provided him with the product or service and he agreed to pay on time. You only want him to keep that promise.

Emails and faxes may be less stressful and both are good ways of sending copies of information but not for collecting. One on one is the most effective way to collect. You can't force anyone to pay you based on a telephone call but you can find out why you have not been paid and what you have to do to get paid. Try to establish a business relationship with the accounts payable staff. They are the front line of defense when a company is having cash flow problems. Make a note of any changes in staffing or management.

Make notes on who you spoke to, what commitment was made and follow up. Customers will keep promises to suppliers who follow up because they know you are someone who will make sure they keep the commitment. It's easier to break promises to the suppliers who don't follow up. Make sure you go over your notes before the follow up call. Don't be intimidated. You have a right to be paid on time. Being organized gives you the advantage, not the customer. He's the one that's past due, not you.

I tell new collectors that collecting is like acting. The chances are that the customer will never meet you so he doesn't know if you're five feet two or six feet ten. Act confidently, don't let him intimidate you and act like you've been collecting money all your life.

Collection Forecasting

Every small, medium sized business owner knows the value of cash forecasting and has probably learned how to prepare an effective forecast. But you need to learn to also forecast collections, by quarter and by month. The principal behind both forecasts is the same; to match revenue to expenses. The collection forecast goes one step further by predicting whether the company will be able to self finance over the next 30-90 days or if it will have to rely on outside sources like a bank for short term working capital. You probably use a spreadsheet to prepare your cash forecast and the same tool can be used for your collection forecast.

Let's look at an example;

Total A/R	Current	1-30days	31-60days	61-90days	>90days
$25,000	$10,000	$8,000	$3,000	$2,000*	$2,000

*includes $1,500 in customer disputes

Current invoices are not likely to be paid in the current month nor are the invoices over 90 days. Customer deductions may be resolved during the month but if you issue credit notes that's a reduction in sales and not cash receipts. Here's how I would forecast collections based on this aging;

Total A/R	$25,000
Less Current	($10,000)
Less >90 Days	($2,000)
Less Disputes	($1,500)
Forecast	$11,500

If your expenses (cash out) are $15,000 for the month, you need to determine where the $3,500 shortfall will come from. If you have cash in the bank or access to a line of credit, you can borrow the money and still pay your fixed costs and salary for the month. But if you've reached your limit at the bank and don't have cash on hand, you need to raise the shortfall from somewhere.

That somewhere can be in the current A/R that you don't otherwise expect to receive. Go through the accounts one by one and see if there are any customers that could pay you this month instead of next month. If the payment is only a couple of days in the future, the customer might agree to provide payment a little sooner. If your collectors have a good working relationship with the customer, they may be able to call in a favour. Are there customers that would issue payment earlier in exchange for an early pay discount or a credit note towards their next order?

After you forecast for a few months you'll get better at it and you will keep finding the slow accounts that are impacting your cash flow by not paying you in the normal business cycle. You may even find that you can reduce your line of credit at the bank and the interest costs that go with it.

Handling Excuses

I go into great detail on how to handle excuses later but for now you should know that excuses fall into two categories;

- the real, legitimate reasons for non-payment. You want to identify and resolve the problem and ask for a partial payment while you're doing that
- **OR** the delaying tactics because the customer can't pay you. You need to control the damage, find out how bad the situation is, try to find a specific solution and timetable and don't hesitate to call in an expert.

Even if you made a mistake on the invoice, short shipped, damaged some product or didn't deliver 100% of the service you promised, you're still entitled to a partial payment while you solve the problem. Arrange for the customer to pay you the part that he agrees he owes you. If you let the customer fully delay payment, you are giving him an interest free loan. Most customers will work with you.

Broken Promises

Broken promises are a sign of poor management or cash flow problems. If the customer continues to break promises you need to take a look at your exposure to the customer. Don't put yourself at risk by granting credit to a customer who can't or won't pay you. If the customer breaks two or more promises to you, go into damage control mode.

If the customer is not co-operating, you can issue a final demand either by fax or email. Tell the customer that you must be paid by a specific date or you will take whatever action you deem necessary to collect in full (see sample demand letter in the index). Depending on your credit application you may be entitled to costs or interest. Don't be surprised if the customer claims that this is the first time he knew there was a problem.

Handling Angry Customers

Customers get angry, use threats and profanity because they are embarrassed to admit that they can't pay you or that they're past due. Instead of accepting their responsibility they try to put you on the defensive. Let the customer burn himself out then calmly remind him why you are calling. Keep bringing the conversation back to the account and that you want to be paid. He will either calm down and make arrangements or admit that he can't or won't pay you.

If the customer gets abusive or threatening, end the call by saying "I'm going to end this call now" and calmly hang up the phone. I won't allow any of my staff to handle threatening or obscene calls from customers and I write that into my procedure and policy.

The reason for the call is not to threaten anyone. If the call gets out of hand, that's when you turn it over to a collection agent.

Hiring, Training and Measuring Credit & Collection Staff

When hiring credit and collection staff, remember that these are the people that will be talking to your customers more often than the rest of your staff, sometimes including sales staff. I can teach someone with customer service skills how to collect. It's much more difficult to teach customer service skills to a collector.

To be a lawyer, you have to pass the bar exam. To be a doctor you have to pass medical exams and intern. Unfortunately the same is not true with credit managers. Anyone can claim to be a credit manager regardless of their background and training. If you're looking for qualified people for your credit and collection functions I would recommend contacting the Credit Institute of Canada (CIC) at www.creditedu.org/ they have some excellent students and credit managers on their rosters. I've been a member for over 30 years. The CIC conducts seminars across Canada throughout the year. I prefer smaller training groups but the Institute does have some good instructors that they work with.

Credit and collection staff is used to being measured by a number of goals;

- days sales outstanding (DSO)
- % of A/R current
- bad debt write offs as a % of sales
- % of last months sales collected
- deductions resolved

Make the credit and collections staff part of your business development process. They usually form a working relationship with the customers and can help identify growth opportunities as well as warning of pending problems. Reward them with some sort of incentive for exceeding the set goals. A few dollars spent with the credit and collections staff will go a long way to helping you grow your business.

Onsite has a small group of trained staff that are available on a contract basis and we have a working relationship with one of Canada's premier placement agencies. I have trained all of our staff myself and their training is included in this guide, especially the collection binder.

I teach new hires that routine collection calls should never be confrontational. The calls are primarily to find out if there is a dispute, when the customer will send payment and to determine if shipping new orders will expose the company to a bad debt loss. The rest of the training is included in the collection template and the responses in the index.

A lot of credit and collections is based on experience and you can't teach that. Credit people need to develop instinct which I call "gut feel" and I always encourage my staff to trust their instincts.

Ian's Big Black Book (how to collect past dues)

When I train people to collect I give them a binder that teaches them the best collection techniques. The binder has often been called Ian's big black book. It's nothing more complicated than a binder divided into days but it's one of the most powerful tools for collecting because it includes all of the specifics I mentioned above and it provides answers to many of the excuses customers use to delay payment. Much of the training material is included in the appendix.

I could write a whole book and still not cover all of the excuses for not paying that I've heard. I'm always amazed by how creative customers are. We've come a long way from "the cheque is in the mail." The most creative excuse I've ever heard was from a customer who told me he couldn't sign cheques because he was an undercover agent for the RCMP and someone might recognize his signature.

My collection techniques are very simple to follow;

1. Find out if the customer disagrees with the balance owing and if so why.
2. Get a specific commitment and follow up.
3. Go over your notes before you call the customer so that you are well prepared.
4. Be persistent but polite and escalate any issues

I've developed a process for collectors to follow when contacting customers. It's basic and easy to use. My staff refer to it as "Ian's Big Black Book" or as "The Collection Bible." The process consists of a three ring binder that is divided into sections 1-31 for each day of the month. In the index I have included a sample template form that you can either copy or use to create your own. On the form is a series of boxes labelled A-J. When a customer gives the collector a reason for not paying or partially paying the account, the collector marks an 'X' in the reason box then refers to the suggested response for that reason.

The following example will help illustrate how the process works;

(i)   On June 1, I call Fred's Trucking & Towing because there is a past due balance of $2,000 on the account

(ii)   I speak to Susan, Fred's wife who tells me that she sent cheque #1955 for $500 by mail the night before.

(iii) I ask her why she is not paying the rest of the past due balance and she says she has no open invoices but if I send her a statement she will mail the rest of the balance Her excuse is index '#H', "I need a statement" so I put an X in that box and refer to my recommended reply in the index which is "**Our terms are based on the invoice date, not the statement date. We**

send you a statement as a matter of courtesy, but you need to pay based on the invoice, not the statement."

(iv) Susan promises to send payment and I enter June 15 as the follow up date and file the form under the section for June 15th in the binder. Notice that I also make a note of the conversation in the notes section.

SEE THE NEXT PAGE FOR THE COMPLETED CONTACT FORM

Because this is the first time I have contacted Susan about the past due balance, I give her 2 weeks to keep her promise.

Contact Section			
Date:	June 1, 2011	Follow Up Date:	June 15, 2011
Phone #:	905-555-1212	Fax #:	905-555-1213
Customer Name:	Fred's Trucking & Towing	Account #:	12345
Who am I speaking to?:	Susan, Fred's Wife	Amount $:	2000

Commitment Section		
How much are you sending / did you send me?	$500	Cheque #1955
When are you sending / did you send it?		May 31, 2011
How are you sending / did you send it?		Canada Post

Important! If a payment has already been sent ask for a cheque number

Resolution Section

Why are you not sending payment (or partial payment)?		Index #
Need Invoice Copy	☐	A
Need Proof of Delivery	☐	B
Pricing Error	☐	C
Did Not Order	☐	D
Short Shipped or Damaged on Receipt	☐	E
Payment Has Not Been Approved	☐	F
Disagree With The Balance Owing	☐	G
I Need a Statement of Account	X	H
Cheque Is Ready But Not Signed	☐	I
Other	☐	J

Notes:
Susan says she needs a statement of account to balance with her payables. I faxed her a statement
and reminded her that payment is due based on the invoice date, not the date she receives her statement
She will mail the balance of $1,500 tomorrow after she receives the statement. She thinks Fred might
have lost the original invoice copies.

On June 15, I open my binder to the form that I filed on June 1. I check Fred's account and find that I haven't received either payment so I call Susan back.

Susan doesn't recall the conversation since she has so many suppliers. I reminder her that she said she sent cheque #1955 on May 31, that I faxed her a statement and she promised to send another $1,500 when she got the statement. Faced with all of that information, Susan admits that she didn't send either cheque. She tells me that Fred lost his largest contract and that the business has cash flow problems. We discuss the situation and Susan makes a new commitment to pay the balance in 2 installments. Because Fred has a new job with another carrier and because the account has been with me for over 5 years, I accept the new promise.

I complete the form and because this is the second commitment I only give Susan one week to keep the new promise. I file the form for follow up on June 22.

On June 22 I check the account and see that Susan kept the promise. We received $500 and post dated cheques for June 30 and July 15. I print out the form and file it in Fred's credit file so that I can refer to it in future.

The process has the added advantage of being user friendly. If I'm not in the office on June 15 or June 22 any one of my staff can pick up my binder and make the same calls that I would make. It's easy to find my notes because they're either 7 or 14 days after my last conversation.

I file the forms in alphabetical order under each follow up date to make them easier to find. You don't have to type in the information on the form, handwriting will do.

The process has the added advantage of providing a tack record of your conversations with the customer in case of a dispute. If you go to small claims court for example, you'll have your notes to refer to.

At one client, I trained 3 collections staff to use my collection binder. Only one collector used it and she was more than 60% more effective at collecting than the other two collectors. In fact, the one collector who used the process was so effective that a competitor hired her away from my client.

SimplyPaid

At the time of writing this guide, I'm working with a programmer to provide a set of programs that will automate the collection process. SimplyPaid will read your receivables file, send past due reminders by letter, fax or email and automatically follow up.

The program will allow you and your staff to track reasons for non payment and provide you with a schedule of when to expect payment. SimplyPaid will be cloud based so you won't need hardware or software. Wherever you have access to the Internet, you'll be able to run SimplyPaid. Best of all, its cost effective.

For more information please visit www.SimplyPaid.ca or email me at ian@onsitecreditgroup.com

Contact Section

Date:	June 15, 2011	Follow Up Date:	June 22, 2011
Phone #:	905-555-1212	Fax #:	905-555-1213
Customer Name:	Fred's Trucking & Towing	Account #:	12345
Who am I speaking to?:	Susan, Fred's Wife	Amount $:	2000

Commitment Section

How much are you sending / did you send me?	$2,000	Cheque #1960
When are you sending / did you send it?		June 15, 2011
How are you sending / did you send it?		Fed-Ex

Important! If a payment has already been sent ask for a cheque number

Resolution Section

Why are you not sending payment (or partial payment)?		Index #
Need Invoice Copy	☐	A
Need Proof of Delivery	☐	B
Pricing Error	☐	C
Did Not Order	☐	D
Short Shipped or Damaged on Receipt	☐	E
Payment Has Not Been Approved	☐	F
Disagree With The Balance Owing	☐	G
I Need a Statement of Account	☐	H
Cheque Is Ready But Not Signed	☐	I
Other	X	J

Notes:

Susan admitted that she has cash flow problems because Fred lost his largest contract.

She has increased her line of credit at the bank based on Fred getting hired on at another carrier

She will send 2 cheques for $1,000 each. One current dated and one for June 30

Dispute or Reconciliation Issues

This is one of the most common excuses used to delay payment and it's one of the hardest issues to argue. If the customer doesn't agree with the balance or claims you applied his payments wrong, you're probably going to have to invest some time and effort to prove that you're right. However, unless the customer is being very difficult, you should ask him to pay you what he agrees that he owes. If your statement says he owes you $1,500 and he says it's only $1,300 ask him for the balance he agrees is owed while you reconcile his account. You don't need to let him delay payment while you research the account. If you do, you're loaning him your money interest free.

If he protests, point out that until he pays you, his account is past due and the balance he owes is using up part of his credit limit so he runs the risk of new orders being put on hold. Remember the part of your policy about shipping to past due accounts?

Managing Customer Deductions

When a customer deducts from his payment to you for shortages, damages, promotions or for a reason he hasn't explained, it can take a lot of time and effort to resolve the deduction and either issue a credit note or collect the short payment. The keys to managing deductions are ownership and visibility.

The important accounting issue is that you want to match deductions to revenue. If you think you are having a great sales quarter but you achieved those sales with a coupon that reduced your prices, you may not recognize that the sales came at the expense of the bottom line if the customer deducts from his payment to you but you don't issue credit notes. If you leave the deduction on the books for months, you could end up with a nasty surprise when you realize that you have to credit or write off those deductions.

Sometimes sales overspends their budget and tells the customer to deduct promotions, price protection or allowances from their next invoice. Sales may intend to use the next budget to clear the deductions but the new budget is used up before the credit notes can be issued. This can become an ongoing issue if left unmanaged. Try to match sales to expenses as closely as possible, including credit notes and deductions.

I keep a separate report of customer deductions and I table the report at every management meeting I attend. I tell my staff that they are responsible for resolving the deduction whether it's a sales, operations or accounting issue. I create a spreadsheet and tell my staff that they own the deduction until it's resolved. I then track the reasons for the deductions and report those reasons and the amount by customer to senior management. I don't want any surprises. Customer deductions are a key component of my SimplyPaid program.

You should include both the aging and the amount of the deduction as part of the credit management of each account. If a customer has a $10,000 credit limit and he has deducted $2,000 from payments to you, that customer only has $8,000 left to buy product or services. If the deductions are over 60 days old, you may want to put the account on hold. Treat an unresolved deduction the same as a past due invoice.

If you leave deductions unresolved for too long you will lose control of the account and increase the risk of a loss. Make sure sales are aware of the deductions so that they can work with the customer to resolve them. It may seem OK to book an accrual to offset the deductions but you need to match the accrual to the debit note and clear it from receivables. Accruals have a way of being reversed when sales or profit margins are soft.

Most importantly don't hide deductions thinking they will go away or that they can be resolved sometime in the future. Deductions are the same as past due invoices and you need to manage them that way.

Workouts

Sometimes your customer will come right out and tell you that they're having cash flow problems. That happened to me a lot during the recession that bankrupted General Motors and Chrysler. Many of my customers weren't being paid and didn't have the cash flow to pay me. My customers wanted to stay in business and needed my help.

If this happens, you must go into damage control mode. You don't have to cut off the customer and you don't have to turn the account over to a collection agency. If you can work with the customer it's usually in your best interest to do so. First, you need to make sure that the customer starts paying down the account. If he wants a new order, have him pay you $2 for every $1 in new orders. Use $1 to pay for the new order and $1 to pay down the old debt. Unless he has given you an NSF cheque in the past, you can probably let him give you an open cheque. If he's given you a bad cheque or you're not comfortable with open cheque, ask for a bank transfer of funds before you ship but still get $2 for every $1 in new orders.

In credit we refer to this kind of situation as a "workout." Often if you help a customer work his way out of a temporary cash flow problem you will earn more of his business in future. *But don't put your self at risk to do so.*

What you should not do is treat the situation as business as usual. If the customer had managed his financials properly, he should be able to go to the bank and borrow enough money to pay his suppliers. After all, the bank is fully secured. If the bank won't loan him more money, why should you?

In extreme cases, the customer may tell you that he will never be able to pay you. If that happens, find out if he has any of your products left. If so, take them back and give him a credit note. Even if you can't get all of your money back, you can reduce your loss. Be careful here since if the customer goes bankrupt you could have a preference. However, I would rather have the product back and argue about it than let someone else have it.

Customer Won't Pay You Until He Is Paid

Customers use this excuse to me all the time. On the credit application it clearly states that payment is due based on the invoice date. Whether the customer has been paid or not has nothing to do with you. You're not in the finance business. If the customer needs to borrow money to pay you until he gets paid, he should go to his bank.

Sometimes the customer will argue that the product you sold to him is part of a project that he has not been paid for yet and that you have to wait until he gets paid. You can be sympathetic but you have no way of knowing if or when he is going to be paid. If his customer takes months to pay him, are you prepared to wait for months?

Point out to the customer that your policy is not to ship to past due accounts and that the unpaid invoice is using up part of his credit limit. You can also point out that he agreed to pay you interest on the past due invoice. If you followed my advice and charged 1.5% per month, the customer will quickly realize that he's better off to borrow the money from the bank. If he can't then you know he has more problems than he admits and you need to reassess the relationship.

Reselling to Delinquent Accounts

If you put a customer on hold, should you re-sell him again on open terms once the account is current? The answer depends on why the account was past due in the first place and how co-operative the customer was in bringing the account current.

Sometimes, businesses get into cash flow problems through no fault of their own. They might have been working on a large contract or installation that was delayed or even cancelled by their customer. They may have had some other, understandable delay beyond their control. Many of my customers were hit hard by the automotive recession in late 2008. They had contracts with GM and Chrysler that were cancelled outright without recourse to recover their costs. Many went under and those that survived took about 2 years to get back on their feet again. By being patient and working with them, I was able to recover most of the money that was owed and in the long run the customers gave us the lion's share of future business because we supported them when other suppliers wouldn't.

It's more expensive to find and develop a new customer than it is to maintain an existing one. If the customer has a genuine reason for paying slow, it may be worthwhile helping him with his cash flow in the short run but not if it puts you at risk. Don't change your credit limit unless you have security and don't change your terms of sale. You can tell the customer that your terms are still net 30 for example but that you understand that he will pay you beyond terms. You can't legally give one customer preferred terms over another, similar customer. By leaving your terms the same but accepting his late payments, you will be operating within the Competition Act of Canada* (see www. competitionbureau.gc.ca As long as you are making progress towards bringing the account current, it may make sense to reinstate terms. See my notes on a workout plan.

Sometimes customers need a wake up call. If you send an internal demand letter (see appendix) it may be enough to get the customer to understand that you are serious about getting paid. However, if the customer ignores your requests and you have to place the account for collection, then future sales should be cash in advance, even if the customer pays you within the free 10 day demand period. If you have to place the account for collection, you are entitled to recover your fees before you sell the customer any product and you are not required to give him terms back. You can tell him you want cash for future product or services and that you want your fees to be included in the first order.

* In lay terms, the Competition Act means that you must treat "like customers alike." If you're not sure that you are compliant I would seek legal advice. When it comes to terms of sale, you need to make sure that all like customers receive the same terms. That's one of the reasons that you include standard terms on your credit application and invoices. If you offer extended terms to one customer you must also offer the same terms to "like" customers. "LIKE" customers include customers who are located in the same geographic area and that buy similar amounts of product or services from you.

I Can't Or I Won't pay You

If the customer comes right out and tells you that you aren't going to be paid then you probably need to turn your account over to someone who makes a living collecting money. You have a business to run and you need to put your efforts into the customers who can and will pay you.

As a credit professional I can tell you that this development in a customer relationship can be devastating. After all at some point in time you trusted the customer when he told you he would pay you. You probably spent a lot of time and energy working to get your money and it's frustrating to have to recognize that you aren't going to be able to collect. It's hard to let go but you have to. There are a lot of good agencies out there who have a different set of skills than you do. Let them go after your money. If the customer tries to contact you, refer him to the agency. Do not try to resolve the account after you place it.

We all second guess ourselves about what we could have done differently. Don't let it interfere with your day to day business. Place the account and move on. You need to work with the rest of your customers who can and will pay you and not let a bad debt affect your ongoing relationships with them.

Except in the case of a fraud, a customer usually doesn't just decide to close his business, lock the doors and walk away. There will be a change in how and when he pays you and there will probably be signs that he's in financial trouble long before the business closes. If you or your staff (including sales) have a sound working relationship with the customer then these signs will be evident. I've had customers actually tell me in advance that they were closing so that I didn't continue to ship new orders.

Selecting a Collection Agency

No matter how effective your collection process is, at some point you will have to place an account with a collection agent in order to get paid. For the agency to be effective, you must turn over the account while there is still a chance to get your money back. Waiting until the account is a year old or has filed for bankruptcy isn't effective.

I recommend that you wait no longer than 60 days after the due date of the invoice. If you've been following my guidelines you have contacted the customer at least three times yet you haven't been paid.

It's always hard to let go of an account because at some point you trusted your customer to pay you. Some customers won't pay you until you bring in a third party. That's how they operate; they use the suppliers' money for as long as possible then move on to another supplier. Eventually they will run out of suppliers but you don't want to be the one that never gets paid.

The sooner you recognize that the customer isn't going to pay you, the sooner you need to turn the account over. If the customer refuses to pay you, turn the account over regardless of how old the invoices are. When you turn over an account, turn over the *entire* balance, not just the past due balance.

The collection agencies have staff that make a living collecting money. They don't get paid unless you do. You need to let them go after your money and get on with running your business.

When selecting a collection agency to use, be sure to pick one that will give you a free 10 day demand period. Sometimes the customer just needs a wake up call to realize that you are serious about getting paid. The agency should be prepared to help you in exchange for getting any accounts that don't pay you within the 10 days. If the agency doesn't offer you a free 10 day demand period, look for another agency.

Collection agents charge fees on a sliding scale basis. They charge a higher fee for small balance accounts, reducing in percentage as the amount increases. If they are collecting from a consumer, they will probably charge you a third of the balance or more since consumer collections are much more difficult. There are no mandated fees and you should be able to negotiate a flat fee or a blended fee. You should expect to pay about 20% on the first $1,000 of your account. Most agencies will not accept claims below a certain amount, usually $100 to $200. I have provided a small dollar demand letter in the appendix for accounts that you can't place with an agency.

If one agent can't collect your account, you can place it with another agent. This is called a second placement, agencies don't like them and your rate will probably be 50%. In some jurisdictions its illegal to have two agencies work on the same account so you will have to formally (and in writing) notify the first agent to close their account and the second agency will want written confirmation.

The agency you select should allow you to place claims online so that they start working the account right away. You should be able to go online and see the status of your claim and correspond with the collector. You should also be able to run reports that show you the status and collectability of all of your files as well as a prediction of how much the agency expects to collect by account.

Most collection agencies have their own in house legal staff. If you have to sue an account, it's probably a good idea to let their legal staff litigate for you. The collector's notes will help them understand the efforts that have been made to collect your account and excuses the debtor has given. If you select another lawyer, you will have to go through the background of the claim and explain what you have done to try and get paid all while the lawyer is charging you by the hour.

Collection agencies are governed by provincial legislation. By law, collection agents have to maintain a trust account. Any payment they get from your customer will be held in trust for up to 30 days before you receive payment less the collection fees. The provincial governments conduct audits of the agencies' trust accounts to make sure that your money isn't being misappropriated. If the trust account is not in order, the agency can lose its license and unfortunately you can lose your money. Be careful which agency you choose.

I work accounts very thoroughly before I turn them over to an agency so they deserve to be paid for any of my money that they recover. When I do turn over an account I want the agency to meet all of my requirements yet charge me the lowest fees. I have contracted with an agency to provide my clients with those same benefits. If you contact me through www.onsitecreditgroup.com I will ensure that you receive excellent service and corporate rates even if you only place one account a year.

Small Claims Court

If, despite your best efforts, your customer still won't pay you and you don't want the expense of placing the account with a collection agency you can sue the customer in one of the Provincial Small Claims Courts.

The courts have repeatedly increased the value of disputes that can be brought to trial in an effort to clear the backlogs in the courts system and to make it easier for small businesses to recover money from debtors who refuse to pay.

The maximum amount differs from court to court;

Province	Maximum Claim Amount
Ontario	$25,000
Manitoba	$10,000
Alberta	$25,000
Newfoundland & Labrador	$25,000
Saskatchewan	$20,000
British Columbia	$25,000
Quebec	$7,000
Prince Edward Island	$8,000
Nova Scotia	$25,000
New Brunswick	$6,000

If you are owed more than the maximum for the province you are in, you can reduce your claim so that it fits under the jurisdiction of the court. For example if your Ontario customer owes you $30,000 you can abandon $5,000 of your claim and sue for $25,000. If you are successful, you can't claim the full $30,000 only the $25,000. Even though you lost $5,000 it may be better than hiring a lawyer and taking it to a higher court. You also can't split your claim into 2 or more actions to keep it below the limit.

To take a debtor to Small Claims Court you don't need a lawyer. You can obtain all of the forms you need online and I have included them in the appendix.

When you go to court you will need your original documents to prove your claim; invoices, proof of delivery, purchase orders, NSF cheque, etc. You should also take the notes of any conversations you have had with the debtor so that you don't have to rely on your memory. Judges like it when you are well prepared and keep detailed notes. If you have followed my collection processes you will be in very good shape to win your case.

When you file your claim, you need to write out a short summary of why the customer owes you the money and attach any documents that prove your claim. You then serve the other party with your claim and the backup documents. The defendant then has the opportunity to respond to your claim. You can either serve the documents on the defendant yourself or pay to have a process server do it for you. I would rather pay the fee to have the papers served for me.

As mentioned, you don't need a lawyer to go to small claims court. You can either represent yourself or hire a law student or a paralegal (I have seen several judges criticize law students for playing lawyer so be careful). In my experience, I usually understand the case better that anyone else so I represent my company at trial. If the lawyer, student or paralegal tells you that you don't have to be there, insist that you be present even if it's just to help the lawyer with some misunderstanding.

You can file your claim either where you conduct business or where the customer has his business. On occasion the court will decide for you but I like to play in my own backyard.

Be careful; if you file in a different province than the one the debtor resides in but where the debt occurred, you may win but your judgment may not be enforceable. For example if you get judgment in Quebec, it is not enforceable in Ontario; you would have to try the case all over again.

As part of the process of increasing the limits, the courts now require a mandatory settlement conference be held to try and settle the dispute before it goes to trial. The conference will either be face to face or by conference call. If a settlement is reached, both parties fill out a terms of settlement form (see appendix) which goes to the court.

If settlement can't be reached, the dispute will go to trial. Although the trial is a legal process it's usually less intimidating than most trials and certainly not as dramatic as Hollywood. It's more Judge Judy than O.J. The judge will hear both sides, look at the evidence and make a decision on who he thinks is right. Judgment may be granted against your debtor and you can ask for both costs and interest (remember your credit application where the customer agreed to pay you costs and interest?). If you hire a lawyer the court will probably not award you his fees since it was your decision to hire him.

Getting judgment does not guarantee that you will get paid but you can now go after any assets the debtor has including bank accounts, wages etc. You can hire the Sherriff to help you once you get judgment. Remember when you ran that D&B or Equifax report? Your judgment will now show up in the credit report that any other supplier orders if the customer applies for credit with other suppliers.

<u>What happens when your customer goes bankrupt?</u>

In Canada, a company can commit one or more acts of bankruptcy yet stay in business. Canadian bankruptcies are governed by Federal laws which have been under attack by trade suppliers for years. Each time we think we are making progress, the government changes and we have to start the process over again.

The most common act of bankruptcy happens when a debtor is unable to meet his debts as they generally come due. If a business is not paying its suppliers then it is committing an act of bankruptcy. As a creditor you have the right to petition the debtor into bankruptcy to prevent him from liquidating the assets of the company but you will need the help of at least two other suppliers. The courts don't like to be used as a collection tool for commercial debts and unless you have at least three suppliers willing to swear that they are not being paid, your petition is likely to fail. If you proceed with a petition you also need to be aware that if there are not enough assets to pay the Trustee's fees then you will be held liable for the fees. If you're considering petitioning a customer into bankruptcy you should seek legal advice.

If your customer makes a proposal, is petitioned into bankruptcy or files for bankruptcy protection you must take immediate action but don't give up entirely on getting some of your money back.

<u>Proposal</u>

If a debtor makes a proposal under the Companies' Creditor Arrangement Act (CCAA) it generally means that he wants to keep his business open and is hoping that his creditors will either take less than the full balance owed or will give him some time to repay the full amount. The customer will go to court and file a plan to repay his creditors over time. The court will usually grant the request provided that there appears to be some chance that the business will stay open and the creditors will get some of their money back. The court gives a great deal of weight to a debtor who appears to be genuinely concerned with repaying his creditors and keeping staff employed.

The court will grant the business a 30 day "stay" during which you can't make a demand for payment, sue or take any other action against the customer. This includes reclaiming product that you have shipped in the last 30 days. (see 30 day goods clause). The court is trying to preserve the assets of the business for the benefit of the creditors as a whole.

A monitor will be appointed to oversee the business and he may or may not call a meeting of creditors to approve his actions. He works for and reports to the court. The monitor or the customer can request an extension of time from the court and there is basically no limit on the number of extensions.

Eventually the monitor will call a meeting to vote on the proposal. Creditors vote in classes; secured, preferred and unsecured creditors. Unless you have a security agreement you will likely be an unsecured creditor. If 50.1% of the unsecured creditors and 2/3 of the dollar value of the unsecured creditors present at the meeting or through proxy vote to accept the proposal, you are bound by that decision even if you voted against it. The key to keep in mind is that it's the outcome of the vote at the meeting that decides. If only a few creditors show up, the vote is still binding on all of the creditors within the class. You can't appeal the decision even if it seems unfair.

If the vote fails, the business is deemed to have become bankrupt *as of the date of the filing of the first proposal* even if that date is months in the past.

Over the past 10-15 years I have seen this section of the Bankruptcy Act abused many times. The debtor may not have had any intention or ability to make a proposal to creditors but wanted to stay in business long enough to liquidate inventory often at distress prices. The real goal of the business owner was to buy time to pay down the secured debt (usually the bank.) By filing an intent to make a proposal the debtor gains 30 days or more during which creditors can't reclaim inventory nor take any action to reduce their exposure. At the end of the 30 days, the debtor either asks for an extension or advises the court that it can't meet the terms of the proposal and files for bankruptcy. Unfortunately there are no consequences to this sleight of hand. The courts will always err on the side of a debtor who appears to be trying to make restitution to its creditors especially if it appears that some or all of the employees will keep their jobs.

Voluntary and Involuntary Bankruptcy

When a company can't meet its obligations to its creditors, it is deemed to be bankrupt. If there is a secured lender like a bank, then the lender will usually go to court to ask for the appointment of a Receiver. Most loans have a provision that grant the secured lender the right to appoint someone whose job it is to safeguard the assets for the benefit of the lender. The Receiver works for the secured lender and will generally do whatever is necessary to get as much of the lender's money back as possible. This will probably include selling your product with or without your knowledge.

The Receiver has no obligation to report his actions to the rest of the creditors that are owed money although he will sometimes issue a report to the creditors at large. Sometimes the Receiver will be successful in recovering all of the money for the lender and he will leave whatever is left of the debtor but in most cases the Receiver will issue a report recommending that the lender appoint a Trustee in bankruptcy.

If one of your customers goes into receivership, you should find out who the receiver is and see if you can work with him to reduce your exposure. If you have an Inventory Security Agreement (ISA) send a copy to the receiver. He can't liquidate your product without your permission. If he does sell it, he has to give you the proceeds of the sale. If you don't have a security agreement, offer to take your product back in exchange for a credit note. You won't be any further ahead but at least you'll keep your products from being sold at fire sale prices.

If the Receiver thinks he can run the business successfully he might ask that you sell new product to him. If so, get a guarantee in writing from the Receivers employer, usually an accounting or auditing form. You may be able to make new sales to help offset potential losses and you may earn the customer's future business if he his able to recover.

In most cases, the damage to the business makes it impossible to recover and bankruptcy occurs. If that's the case there is little that you can do except file a proof of claim (see sample in the index). However you don't have to abandon your claim entirely. I have been involved with bankrupt estates that paid up to 80% of the total owing to unsecured creditors. General Motors and Chrysler repaid billions of dollars back to the Canadian and U.S. Governments.

If you can, attend the meeting of creditors. Don't expect that the debtor is going to confess that he's been hiding money in a Swiss bank account and that he's now going to pay you back. But, you can learn a lot about what causes bankruptcies and how to avoid them by attending the meeting and participating. In every meeting I've attended, I've met someone who knew that the bankrupt was having problems but didn't know who else to talk to about the information they had. Try to network with other suppliers, especially the ones in your own line of business.

Filing a proof of claim is very straightforward but if you make mistake, you can void your claim and right to vote. Never sign a proxy unless you are providing the vote to someone you know and trust. If you sign the proxy over to the Trustee, you are stuck with however he votes whether it's in your favour or not. At Onsite Credit we work with our clients to make sure they are properly represented in bankruptcies.

The bankruptcy code can be very intimidating with its threats of fines and sanctions but you don't have to surrender your position completely. If you have a dispute with the Trustee, play hard ball. The Trustee will take the easy way out to recover the most money for whoever appointed him. If that's the bank then he'll sell the inventory first and go after receivables next. If he thinks you owe the estate money he'll try to get you to pay the money into the estate.

On the proof of claim you're required to list any payments that you received and credits you have issued within the 3 months before the bankruptcy. I would not volunteer this information, even if you took back product just before the bankruptcy. The Trustee will accuse you of having a preference and will demand that you repay the estate. I would prefer that you maintain that you have the first right of offset against the balance that the bankrupt owes you. If you go to court, the Trustee will win but in my experience that seldom happens. The Trustee will take the low hanging fruit and once he has paid back the secured creditor he will move on. He certainly does not want to get into litigation.

There is always the risk that the Inspectors instruct the Trustee to go after you for repayment but that seldom happens. Once you have your money or product, never voluntarily give it back.

Your 30 Day Goods Rights

Prior to changes in the Bankruptcy and Insolvency Act (BIA) only suppliers in the province of Quebec had the right to repossess product shipped within 30 days of an insolvency. The suppliers' rights in Quebec dated back to the Napoleonic Code (yes that Napoleon) and later the Quebec Civil Code.

Suppliers and the Credit Institute of Canada successfully lobbied the federal government to change the BIA so that all suppliers have the right to repossess product shipped 30 days immediately preceding an insolvency.

Before the change, insolvent debtors were maximizing their credit limits with suppliers to build up inventory prior to filing for bankruptcy. The reason for bulking up inventory was to increase the assets for the bank and in some cases this was done with the knowledge of the banker. The bank takes inventory as part of its general security and the more inventory there is, especially new inventory, the better for the bank. Earlier in the guide, I suggested that you be careful if the customer's buying habits suddenly change.

If your customer files for bankruptcy or is placed into receivership, you have the right to demand the return of your product *provided* that the following guidelines are met;

- your customer must already be in bankruptcy or receivership,
- you need to submit, within 30 calendar days of **delivery of the product** a notice of claim (see form 75 in the appendix) to the trustee or receiver,
- your product must be in the trustee or receiver's possession (usually in inventory),
- your invoices for the product must be unpaid but not necessarily past due,
- your product must be in as shipped condition and you have to be able to prove that its your product

Once the trustee or receiver agrees to allow you to take back your product you have to do so within 10 days at your own expense. If you don't want to take the product back you can offer it for sale to the trustee or receiver. If you do then he will be able to sell it at whatever price he wants which might be at a price below what your other customers are paying you for the same product.

The trustee or receiver has a fiduciary responsibility to notify all known creditors within a legislated timeframe. In the case of a bankruptcy that means within 5 days; in a receivership it means 10 days. You need to remember that the trustee or receiver is working for a secured creditor, usually the bank and the more inventory he has to sell, the more his client is going to recover and the more fee the trustee is going to earn.

You must prove that any product in the trustee or receiver's possession is yours and is not paid for. The best way to prove that is by having serial numbers on your invoices (not on the packing slip or bill of lading). You can then compare the serial numbers on the invoice to the serial numbers in inventory. If you shipped 10 units on an invoice and 2 have been sold, you are only entitled to repossess the remaining 8.

I've had cases where I've argued that since my client was the sole manufacturer of the product in inventory that there was no need to provide serial numbers but that's a difficult argument to win (I did win). Keep in mind who is paying the trustee's fees.

The trustee or receiver may argue that your products are not "in their original state" but simply taking product off a pallet and putting it on a shelf does not change your rights to possession. I would argue that an open box does not change your rights either but I might lose that argument.

Your rights to repossession can be frustrated if the customer files an intent to make a proposal (see my notes on proposals) since the court will grant a stay. Proposals fall under a different legislation called the Companies' Creditor Arrangement Act (CCAA) and there are more filings under CCAA than under the BIA.

Whether you can prove the shipment date or that the product is yours and has not been paid for, I recommend that you file a form 75 anyway. Trustees and receivers don't like arguing and will avoid litigation so you may get some of your goods back. It doesn't hurt to ask.

Stoppage in Transit

If you find out that one of your customers is in bankruptcy or receivership while the product is en route you have the right to contact the carrier and instruct them not to deliver the goods to the customer. You can have the product returned to you or stored in a third party warehouse.

I did this once and the customer argued that the product was FOB my warehouse so title transferred to him once it was put on the truck. My answer to him? "Sue Me!" he didn't.

First Right of Offset (Setoff)

If you owe an insolvent customer money for any reason (i.e. a partial prepayment or deposit, co-op or advertising funds) you have the right to offset what you owe to the customer against what the customer owes you. If you end up owing the customer money, wait for the trustee or receiver to serve you with a claim.

The right of offset extends to Revenue Canada as well. I had a customer that I owed money to for warranty work he did for my company. He was not paying us so in turn we weren't paying him, It turned out that he owed Revenue Canada for sales tax that he had collected but not remitted. Revenue Canada served me with a demand to pay them the money I owed to the customer. I successfully argued that I had the right of offset. The customer later went bankrupt but I had all of my money.

Do you need a lawyer to represent you at a bankruptcy hearing?

No, in fact I would recommend against it. You're already at risk of losing all or part of you account. It makes no sense to add legal costs. Meetings of creditors follow a legislated process that likely can't be influenced by legal council. There is nothing he can do at the meeting that you can't do for yourself.

A Trustee in bankruptcy will conduct the meeting according to the Bankruptcy Act which is a federal statute. He is a court appointed officer who is responsible for maximizing the return for the benefits of all of the creditors. Granted, he's being paid by the secured creditor (usually the bank) but by the time he calls the meeting most of the assets have been sold off. The Trustee has a duty to follow the Act and if he does not, he can be fined or lose his license.

Here's what happens at the first meeting of creditors. Before the meeting starts you must file your proof of claim or a proxy letter (see my comments below) or you won't be allowed to vote. The Trustee will call the meeting to order and advise the number of proofs of claim and proxy letters that he has received. He will read his report on what happened to cause the bankruptcy and what he has done to recover the funds for the creditors. He should have examined the business owners who may or may not be at the meeting.

If the owners are present you have the right to ask them any reasonable question you want about the business but don't expect them to confess their sins and give you a cheque. The meetings often get emotional especially if there are ex-employees present. One or two creditors may become angry since they trusted the bankrupt with their money.

If there's a chance that some or all of the money can be recovered the Trustee will include that in his report and may ask for approval to sell or dispose of assets. Usually however the Trustee has already exhausted his efforts and he'll advise his recommended next steps. He's looking for approval from the creditors which is why you have to be able to vote.

The Trustees are accountants, not businessmen and you probably know more about the bankrupt company's business than he does. He'll ask the suppliers who are present to help him maximize the return for everyone by volunteering to act as Inspectors in the estate. There does not have to be any Inspectors and there is a maximum of 5. Inspectors are required to help the Trustee on behalf of everyone and can't act in their own best interests if it harms everyone else.

Even if you don't intend to be at the meeting, you must file a proof of claim in order to vote. You can assign your right to vote to the Trustee or someone else to vote on your behalf but you then have to hope that he votes the way you want. I generally do not complete the proxy.

If you don't file your claim in time to attend the meeting, you can still participate in any dividend as long as you file your proof of claim before the dividend is paid out.

Think it's a waste of time to file a proof of claim? As of May 2011 there are unclaimed funds of just under $15 million according to the Office of the Superintendent of Bankruptcy Canada. The largest single amount is $179, 636.00. I was an Inspector in a bankruptcy that recovered over $1 million for the unsecured creditors.

Vulture Funds

A vulture fund is a private equity fund that buys up the debt of distressed companies at a discount in the hopes that the company will repay some or all of its debt. Vulture funds often approach unsecured creditors of an insolvent company to sell their claim against the estate at a discount in the hope that the estate will recover more than the Fund paid out. Earlier this year I was asked to sell a client's claim against Visteon, a General Motors subsidiary. I declined because the offer was conditional upon too many factors. Three weeks later Visteon advised me that they were paying the full balance.

If you are approached by a Vulture Fund to sell your claim, be sure to weigh the offer against the likelihood that you will be paid a dividend from the estate. The Trustee's fees may be considerable and the Fund is usually offering payment now and not sometime in future.

Setting a Reserve for Doubtful (Bad Debt) Accounts

No matter how thorough or careful you are in granting credit and collecting, you *will* have bad debts. How you plan for and manage your reserve will have a direct impact on your cash flow and probably your bottom line as well. I recommend that you set a bad debt reserve either quarterly or every six months.

Reserves are generally set in one of two ways;

1. A Specific Reserve
   - if a customer has told you that he can't or won't pay you the amount owing you should include a reserve for the entire balance until you can work out a repayment plan
   - if you have turned an account over to a collection agency or a lawyer then you should reserve the balance in full
   - any balances over 90 days past due by customer should also be included
   - if, based on your knowledge of the customer you have reason to believe that you won't be paid in full, you should include at least a portion of the balance until you resolve any disputes

2. A General Reserve
   a. you can set aside a percentage of your total accounts receivable based on your historical bad debt experience. For example if you have written of 0.50% of your sales over the past 3-5 years then you can set aside 0.50% of your total accounts receivable
   b. you can then also add any specific account that you determine can't or won't pay you

There are accounting guidelines to follow but if you have set your reserve properly then your accountant should be able to follow your logic and approve the reserve. Proper accounting procedure is to match expenses to revenue. The reserve is a reduction in income and a balance sheet item that will reduce your accounts receivable. Revenue Canada may want to know how you arrived at your reserve since it reduces your taxable income. You can't continue to accumulate reserves in order to minimize taxes.

Not setting a reserve can have significant affect on your cash flow and profits. If you run out of money because your customers aren't paying you then you may have to borrow to pay your expenses until you can make more sales and hopefully get paid

Types Of Bad Debt Losses

There are 2 kinds of bad debt losses;

   - an unavoidable loss happens when the customer was current, within the credit limit and there was no information available that would have caused you to consider the customer a bad debt risk
   - an avoidable loss happens when you continue to grant credit to a customer who was past due, over the limit or you ignored information that would have warned you of a bad debt risk

I'm very hard on my staff if they continue to have avoidable losses. I include in my procedure and policy that staff who continue to expose the company to bad debt losses will be disciplined up to and including dismissal.

The True Costs of Bad Debt Write Offs

At 10% gross margin, a bad debt write off of $10,000 requires new sales of $100,000 to recover the cost of the write off

At 5% gross margin, a write off of $10,000 requires new sales of $200,000 to recover the cost of the write off.

The new sales will only cover the cost of the bad debt write off; they will not create new profits.

SECTION 4

Tips, Tricks & Suggestions

Tips, Tricks and Suggestions

In this section I'll share some of the tips and tricks that I've learned over the years, most of them the hard way. You don't have to read through this section in detail. You can refer to it as the various situations come up. I'll also provide some suggestions on how to respond to various issues.

Are you responsible for the customers' delinquency?

Your terms of sale are stated on your invoices or statement. You are under no obligation to provide past due notices, reminder calls, invoice copies or faxes to remind the customer that his account is past due. If you do follow up, it's as a convenience to the customer and he should not wait for a collection call before he decides to pay you.

The customer asked for terms which you granted. He then issued a purchase order which you filled with products or services and he should pay you based on the terms he agreed to. If he has an open purchase order that does not have a receiving or invoice to match then he should investigate instead of waiting for his suppliers to call him about arrears on the account.

I generally comply with requests for POD and invoice copies but I gently remind my customer that I'm doing him a favour. If the pattern persists I will pull the credit file and do a review.

Getting Past Voice Mail

A lot of people don't answer their phone any more especially if they're hiding from suppliers. They let calls go to voice mail then only return the ones they want to.

I had a customer who would never answer his phone and never called me back. I left him detailed messages about the $5,000 that he owed me but I never got a return call. One day I left a message that said, "I'm calling you about the $15,000 that you owe me. Please call me back to-day." He called within 15 minutes saying "I only owe you $5,000 not $15,000!" I told him that I was sorry for my mistake but now that I had him on the phone we needed to talk.

Late Return of Voice Mail;

One customer would always return my calls after he knew I had gone home for the day. That way I could never accuse him of not returning my calls. I solved that problem by staying late one night so that when he called I picked up the phone. He was surprised and disappointed.

Getting Around the Switchboard Gatekeeper

A lot of companies have their switchboard screen calls and keep suppliers from getting to decision makers. I had a customer John P who never accepted calls. I had reason to believe that his company was having problems and I wanted to get my money out. Putting the account on hold and emailing John had no effect so one day I called and was told he was in a meeting. I told the operator that I would hold. She came back on every few minutes but I told her I would continue to hold.

I then had each of my staff call on John's other lines and tell the switchboard that they also would hold. We tied up all of the lines in and out of John's company until he came to the phone.

I got my money, John's company went bankrupt several months later, and John was charged with fraud and left the country.

How to Cash Post Dated Cheques

If month end is on a Friday but your customer gives you a cheque post dated for the next day which is a Saturday you can still deposit the cheque apply the payment and not have the cheque returned as post dated.

To do this you have to damage the cheque. At the bottom of every cheque there is a unique series of numbers called the Magnetic Ink Character Recognition (MICR) code. It's the Transit Number, Institution Number and Account Number that belongs to the bank account that the cheque is written on. Bank machines read the MICR number at very high speeds with a failure record of less than 1%. The machines are able to read the MICR number even if someone writes over them.

If you get a cheque that is post dated to the next day, you can still deposit it, apply the payment and bring a customer current. To do this, punch a hole in part (but not all) of the MICR so that the machine can't read the code automatically. The cheque will be rejected and put aside to be processed manually, at the end of the day. Banks close off the business day usually at 3:00 PM. When the center has closed off for the day, the cheques that are rejected will be processed by hand but by then the date has been changed to the next business day which is either the Saturday or the Monday. The post dated cheque is now dated for the right day. You've had use of the funds and your account is now current. Very few banks return cancelled cheques to the client so your customer will probably never know.

I wouldn't try this if the cheque is post dated more than one or two days beyond the deposit date.

Accepting Payment by Credit Card

If it's your business practice to let customers pay you by credit card and you do not get an original signature on the credit card transaction, you are at risk of the credit card company reversing the transaction up to 90 days after you process the charge.

Electronic payments are very common in our daily lives. You can reduce your risk by having the customer fax you written permission to use the card. The customer should sign the fax. Depending on the size of the order you may also want him to include photo ID so that you can verify that he is the card holder. I would recommend that you have a maximum amount that you will ship without an original signature. If you're in doubt, ship the order with instructions that the customer must provide valid ID when paying by credit card on delivery. That transfers the risk from you to the carrier.

I don't allow customers to pay past due invoices by credit card. Why not? Because I've already carried the account for at least 30 days which probably cost me about 0.50% interest. If I then have to pay the credit card fee on top of that, I am increasing my expense and reducing my net income. If the customer wants credit card terms then the order should be approved before it ships. Some customers want the points from their credit card and I offer them the option of paying the credit card fees so they can get the points. Very few customers accept my offer.

Exception: I <u>will</u> accept a credit card to avoid a bad debt or as a replacement for an NSF cheque but I insist that the customer provides me with written approval to charge his credit card.

COD Shipments

There is case law in Canada that states that "COD" means Cash On Delivery. If you ship product to a customer on a COD basis because you believe that you might not get paid otherwise, the carrier by law must collect cash. That means that even if the carrier gets a certified cheque from your customer on delivery, you are not paid until the cheque clears the customer's bank. If the payment that the carrier gets on delivery is returned for any reason, you have recourse against the carrier who may be better able to pay you than the customer.

The reason that the carrier is liable is because he charges you a COD fee. The Courts have ruled that only cash on delivery meets the legal definition of COD. If the carrier accepts a cheque, even a certified cheque on delivery, he is doing so for his own convenience and the liability now switches to the carrier. If you don't get paid for a COD shipment, file a claim against the carrier and let him go get your money from the customer.

Providing Replacement Invoices

I explain in detail later how to overcome the excuse of having to provide an invoice copy before getting paid. However there are times when the customer insists that you provide an original invoice copy even though the original was already sent. This is usually done for audit purposes and some customers won't pay based on a fax or email copy of the invoice.

You can overcome this problem by reprinting the invoice and writing on the copy "This is a certified true copy of the original invoice." Then date and sign the invoice. This will meet any audit requirements including if your customer is using the invoice as part of his financing with the bank or a third party. A certified invoice copy is just as legal as the original.

Restrictive Endorsement

Never leave customer cheques lying around without stamping them with your company stamp on the reverse or writing "Deposit to the credit of . . ." Leaving unendorsed cheques where someone can get them is an invitation to fraud or theft.

Anyone can take those cheques and deposit them into their bank account. Because of the volume of cheques they handle every day, the banks and credit unions don't check to see if the person who deposited the cheque is the same person that the cheque is payable to.

The banks rely on you to discover the fraud and report it to them. You won't know about the theft until you call your customers and they send you a copy of the cashed cheque. That could be months later.

If you work with the customer and your bank you can usually get your money back but that takes many weeks or months and you have to swear a statement that you did not receive the original cheque.

I've seen several cases of this during my career. Someone takes the cheques and deposits them to their bank account and almost always gets caught and almost always the person has left the company before the police arrive. They may even have left the country. When charges are laid, there is seldom any real punishment handed out by the courts.

Another way to avoid bank fraud is through segregation of duties. The person who handles the original cheques should not be the same person that makes the deposit and should not be the same person that handles your cash application. If you don't have enough staff for segregation of duties, make sure someone stamps the cheques and lists the cheques or makes copies of them. That will speed up your investigation.

Another way to avoid theft is through a lockbox which I cover in another section of the manual.

Warning Signs

Except in the case of out and out fraud, companies don't normally lock their doors and steal off into the night. There are a number of warning signs that your customer may be having financial problems. Your sales staff can watch for some signs while your accounts receivable staff can pick up other clues.

Watch for holes on the shelves where product should be especially in a retail environment. If you notice that your customer does not have all of the lineup in products that he should have, it may be because a supplier has him on credit hold. This is especially true if the missing supplier is a key vendor in your industry. When I was at Hitachi I got worried if I didn't see any Sony product on the shelf.

If the boxes on the shelf are empty, the customer could be trying to represent that he has stock from several suppliers when in fact he may be on hold with one or more. Have your salesman check both the stock on the floor and any boxes that are in inventory.

If you find out that your customer is selling product below cost, even if it's not yours, be concerned. No one survives long by selling below cost (cost includes any co-op, rebate or sales incentive).

If the owner suddenly changes his lifestyle from a penny pincher to become a high roller, he may be doing it with your money.

Keep in touch with your customer's other suppliers. If they tell you about a sudden change in payment patterns or NSF cheques you should look at your account.

If you notice a large staff turnover at your customer try to find out what the cause is, especially if the staff is in accounts payable. Payable staff are often under stress when a company is managing its cash flow.

If the customer significantly changes the volume he buys from you, find out why.

If you were always able to speak to key employees but find they are no longer accessible there may be a reason.

Postal Strikes

Mail strikes are an unfortunate part of doing business in Canada and you will be affected whenever there is a strike. However, you don't have to wait until the strike is over to get paid. During a strike you can get your customers to pay you in several ways that don't involve Canada Post. In fact, during postal strikes I usually get paid faster than normal.

Bank transfers are the most common method of payment along with Electronic Funds Transfers (EFT). In both cases you only need to provide your customer with the name and address of your bank, the transit number and the account number. Payments can be made without the customer leaving his office. The customer may resist but be firm and tell him that you will pay any bank fees (there are usually none) in exchange for his help in getting you paid. You may even consider a discount for an EFT since not only will you get paid, but there is no risk of a bank transfer being NSF.

You can also use your staff to deliver invoices and pick up cheques or if the cheque is large enough send a courier. Most large companies set up a pick up location for vendor cheques. Make sure your employee has identification along with a letter or memo on letterhead authorizing him to pick up your cheques. Remember when I suggested getting an email address for accounts payable on the credit application? Now is when that pays off. You can scan and email your invoices until the strike is over.

Some customers may complain that they are not being paid and in turn expect you to wait for your money. It may sound like poor customer service, but the strike is not your fault and the customer is obligated to pay you on time regardless of whether or not they are being paid. Now is the time to reward the customers who have been paying you on time by giving them prompt payment discounts or some extra flexibility to thank them for paying you on time. It's also a good time to earn some goodwill and extra business in future. If you offer a discount, giving the customer a couple of extra days will help him but you still need your money before the due date or you can't offer the prompt pay discount.

I would not charge interest on past due accounts during a postal strike but I would not allow unearned prompt payment discounts either. The discount is for paying the invoice before the due date. There are a number of ways that the customer can do that so he should not expect to pay late and still get his discount.

Most importantly don't adjust your credit limits during the strike. Yes, you will have more customers who exceed their credit limit and that will put extra strain on your order process but the limit is there for a purpose. The customer does not become less of a credit risk during a postal strike. In fact, if he does not manage his cash flow properly, the strike could put him out of business. There is also a risk that you forget to reset the limits after the strike.

If your customers need additional working capital during a mail strike, encourage them to go to the bank.

When is a cash discount earned?

If you offer your customers a discount for paying you before the due date of the invoice, by law the customer has earned the discount on the day that the payment was received by Canada Post regardless of how long it takes for you to receive the cheque.

Most customers have their own postage meter and the internal postage date and the Canada Post date should usually be within one or two days of each other. If you find there is more than that, it may be because the customer is running the envelope through their own meter then setting aside the cheque to manage cash flow before actually mailing the payment.

Canada Post takes meter abuse very seriously and there are fines and confiscation of postage meters for any company caught cheating the mail dates. If you suspect that your customer is doing that, keep the original envelopes and confront the customer with the evidence. They will usually stop and should repay you any unearned discounts taken.

Not Sufficient (NSF) Cheques

Let me state very clearly that I *hate* NSF cheques. Why? Because a returned cheque for non sufficient funds means not only does the customer not have enough money in the bank, but it also means that the bank will not loan the customer any more money. That puts all of the risk on me.

I do understand that sometimes the customer makes a mistake or the bank makes an error but an NSF cheque is a very clear warning sign to an unsecured creditor. Often the customer will tell me that the bank made a mistake and will even provide a letter from the bank apologizing for the returned cheque but it does not change the fact that when the cheque was presented there was not enough money in the account.

Regardless of the reason that the cheque was returned, until you replace it, you have a risk of a loss. The banker has told you that he's not willing to lend the customer any more money and you can be sure that the bank's fully secured including personal guarantees from the owners of the company.

If the customer offers to provide you with a replacement, ask for a certified cheque or a direct deposit. Taking an open cheque to replace an NSF cheque leaves you in the same position since a cheque is only a promissory note and not payment. Don't take a series of post dated cheques unless you are in a workout situation which I covered earlier. If the customer won't give you a certified replacement you can always take the new cheque to his bank and ask that it be certified (you will be charged a small fee) or you can send the cheque to your bank "on collection" and ask your bank to notify you when it clears.

I make it a practise to charge a returned cheque of at least $25.00 which covers my own bank fees and sends a clear message to the customer that I won't tolerate NSF cheques.

Once I get an NSF cheque I go into damage control mode. I stop all shipments and put new orders on hold. I tell the salesman that I have an issue that I need to resolve but I do not tell the salesman that I have an NSF cheque until I have a chance to speak to my customer. Sales staff has a tendency to overreact to NSF cheques and the damage to the customer's reputation can be significant. The customer is already embarrassed and he doesn't need to think that I'm telling the whole world about his problems. At the same time, I don't need to put myself more at risk by shipping new orders.

NSF cheques are caused either by poor management or a lack of working capital. Before I consider reinstating credit terms I want to know which one it is. I do a complete review of the credit file and will almost always ask for financial statements. It may seem like I'm overreacting but my experience has been that a customer who issues NSF cheques has an underlying financial problem. I will work with a customer who has cash flow problems and needs time to pay me, but the customer should not issue cheques when he knows or suspects that he has no money.

Note: It is a common misconception that issuing NSF cheques is an act of fraud. Although issuing cheques with no money in the bank is a serious matter, it's almost never done on purpose and can easily be defended by a customer admitting that he does not reconcile his bank accounts and thought he had money in the bank. If the customer can show that he had a balance close to the amount at the time he issued the cheque, there will be no basis for alleging fraud. Stupidity is a viable defence against an allegation of fraud.

A small trick;

I had a customer that gave me an NSF cheque that his bank would not certify because it was $10.00 short. Instead of giving up, I deposited $10.00 of my own money into the customers account and the bank then had to certify the cheque.

Lockboxes

A lockbox is really a mail box address that customers send cheques to instead of sending them to you. The mail box is administered by your bank and the cheques are deposited directly into your account for immediate use. Depending on the level of service you have, the bank will then provide you with the backup from the customer as well as the original envelope.

Lockboxes are more popular in the U.S. than here in Canada because of the way the U.S. banking system works. Customers who want to delay payments often open bank accounts that are on the opposite side of the country from where the business is located. For example a New York based company may open a California bank account because under U.S. banking rules the cheque has to find its way from New York to California before being cleared. Lockboxes are however becoming common place here in Canada.

If you want to pay the fees, the bank will apply the payments for you but they charge per cheque as well as per keystroke for their keypunch operators. The bank knows which of your accounts the cheque belongs to based on the unique MICR code on the bottom of the cheque but there is no electronic way to apply the cheque to your invoices other than by data entry.

You can expect to pay upwards of $100.00 per month for a lockbox but you save the expense of someone going to the bank to make the deposit. You also eliminate the risk of someone endorsing your cheques and depositing them in their bank account.

Deflecting the Blame

Past due customers will try to deflect the discussion away from their past dues, claiming that there must be other customers that are past due. Keep bringing the customer back to the conversation by saying "we're not talking about other customers; we're talking about your account."

Threatening to Take Business Elsewhere

Yes, I get this all the time. "If you don't take my account off hold I'm going to take my business to your competitor." This is where your procedure and policy comes in. If you are staff, tell the customer that you are only following procedure and policy and that you are not authorized to take the account off hold until it is current. If the customer gets upset or angry you can buy yourself some time by saying that you will escalate the decision to senior management (or the owner unless of course you are the owner). If you're the business owner you can make an exception to the policy but make sure the customer understands that *it is an exception* and not the way you normally do business

Whatever decision is made make sure that you call the customer back and tell them what has been decided. The customer needs to know that he can't go over your head every time he does not like your decision.

If the customer is not satisfied with your decision, you can only tell him that it's his choice to place the order with someone else and that you understand and respect that decision. There's a good chance that he's on hold with the other suppliers as well.

A cheque is not payment

It might surprise you to know that a cheque is not payment. It is in reality a promissory note. You are only paid after the funds are withdrawn from the customer's bank account and deposited into your account. In between, the cheque can be stop paid, returned as NSF or dishonoured by the customers bank for a number of reasons including account closed, not authorized, funds frozen, body and figures etc.

If your customer is a high risk or has a history of returned cheques, you should not consider your account paid until the funds are actually in your bank account. If you're not sure, contact your bank, give them the details of the cheque and ask them to verify when the cheque has been cleared. You can also take the cheque to your bank and place it on collection which means the bank will call you once the funds are cleared.

There is a general opinion that knowingly issuing cheques without the funds to cover is a crime. In Canada it is a misdemeanor that is easily defended by pleading stupidity. If you sue a customer for giving you an NSF cheque, all the customer has to prove is that he had enough to cover the cheque in his bank around the time that he gave you the cheque. He can claim that he didn't reconcile his account but thought he had the money on hand. Stupidity is a viable defense against issuing NSF cheques.

Credit Fraud

Commercial fraud is an unfortunate part of doing business. Because a lot of fraud never gets reported it's impossible to determine the exact cost but the Canadian government estimates that a typical company loses 5% of its annual revenue to fraud and the average loss is $160,000.

Commercial fraud falls under the jurisdiction of the RCMP; www.rcmp-grc.gc.ca/ccb-sddc/index-eng.htm which has 30 commercial fraud crime stations across the country. They are understaffed and only investigate frauds in the multi million dollar range. Even then, you have to do most of the background checking yourself before they take any interest. The challenge in alleging fraud is that you have to prove *intent*. Not only do you have to prove that the customer defrauded you, but you have to prove that he deliberately set out to do so.

The best way to avoid becoming a victim is through prevention. I've been victimized by fraud twice in my career. In one case I should have known better and in the other case there was no way to avoid a loss. Here are the cases that I was involved in and the lessons I learned from each;

Case #1

I had just started in the electronics industry and had no real knowledge of the customers. Our Montreal salesman placed an order for a new account. The salesman gave me a Dun & Bradstreet report, a bank report and three credit reference faxes that the customer had provided to him because the account had to be opened within 24 hours or we would lose the sale. The order was for 50 Blue Ray DVD players which were very expensive when they first came on the market. When I pointed out to the salesman that the customer didn't sell electronics, he told me that the DVD players were promotional items for the employees.

The D&B report was excellent, the bank reference was sound and all three reference letters stated that the customer had a track record of paying on time. I opened the account and approved the order.

A month later when the invoice hadn't been paid I called the customer and found out that the phone was out of service. I asked the salesman to check on the customer and he reported back that the building was empty. The neighbours told him that the customer packed everything in the middle of the night into one trailer and told everyone they were moving the company from Montreal to Toronto. The trailer never made it out of Quebec neither did the driver who disappeared and has never been found.

It turned out that the D&B report was forged as was the bank report and the reference faxes. Lessons learned;

-   don't accept credit reports, bank reports or trade references if they are presented by the customer unless you independently confirm the data
-   if the customer needs the account opened immediately ask why (beware of the "gotta have" which may include your own sales staff)
-   if the product ordered does not make sense for the customer's business, ask why

Case #2

One of my customers was in the business of renting high end audio and video equipment for concerts and business conferences across Canada. To save on overhead, the customer consolidated several branches from various provinces into one head office in Montreal. More than $1 million in inventory was shipped from the branches to the head office location. When I visited the customer as part of my due diligence I asked about damages and shortages since the product was very high end electronics. The V.P. of Finance showed me his inventory adjustment entry in the general ledger. Less than $1,000 was damaged primarily because the equipment was shipped in specially designed crates. I toured the premises and personally saw the product in inventory and in the process of being staged for an upcoming concert in Ottawa.

Soon after my visit the company filed for bankruptcy protection and offered to sell the assets at auction. Several potential buyers visited the head office location to bid on the inventory but there was less than $100,000 in product on site. The company claimed that the inventory had gone missing when it was shipped from the branches. Since there was no inventory there was only one bidder, the officers of the company who offered suppliers a lump sum of $100,000.

At the bankruptcy meeting, I was appointed an Inspector and immediately instructed the Trustee to sue the officers of the company for fraud. The case has not yet come to trial more than 10 years later. As part of the investigation it was determined that the company shipped the inventory to a third party warehouse then brought it back after successfully buying it for 10% of its value.

In a case like this, there was nothing that I could have done differently. There are some very intelligent people out there who are determined to defraud their suppliers and they are smart enough to find new ways of doing it all the time.

<u>Drop Shipments</u>

One method of fraud that has become quite easy is to have suppliers drop ship product to a location that is not a legitimate company. When the supplier tries to recover the product it turns out that the drop shipment address is a fraud.

If you get a drop shipment order you can verify the address through Canada Post at www. canadapost.ca/segment-e.asp If you enter the address Canada Post will identify the location for you. If it does not appear to be a legitimate address, be careful about shipping the product.

I've had cases where the customer asked for the product to be delivered to the lobby of a building where a fake employee signs for the goods then disappears. Quite often the customer has a taxi driver deliver the shipment because a courier will ask for ID but the cabbie only wants his fare and doesn't care who accepts the delivery.

<u>How Many Accounts Can A Collector Handle?</u>

If you're hiring staff or considering adding staff to handle your credit and collection functions, how do you determine how many staff you need? The answer depends largely on the type of customer that you have. If you have a few, large accounts that have only a few invoices outstanding then you may not need a large credit staff. However if you have hundreds or even thousands of accounts, you may need several people.

Here are my two rules of thumb;

1. Credit management is management by exception. I don't care about the customers that pay me on time; I care about the customers that don't pay within terms. If you use the 80/20 rule you'll be more right than wrong. If you have 1,000 active accounts then your staff will probably have to manage 200 of those accounts. To be effective at collecting your staff will probably need to make 2 calls per month to the customers; the first one to get a commitment and the second one to follow up. That means an average of 400 calls in a month for someone that does nothing else but call for money. An average collection call should last about 5 minutes but the customer will have reconciliation issues, proof of delivery requests, will need invoice copies etc so the average call will be closer to 10 minutes. Based on my experience a full time collector (who has no input into setting credit limits or approving orders) should be able to manage about 500 accounts.
2. I am a very strong believer in ownership and accountability and don't like to split my staff into one group that handles credit approvals and releases orders and another group that just dials for dollars. I prefer my staff to open the account, approve the credit limit, OK the orders and then collect for any past due invoices. That way they get to understand every facet of the customer and become a true business partner. Under those guidelines I've found that 250-300 is about the right number of accounts for a staff member to manage.

<u>How To Say No Without Losing The Sale</u>

There is always the risk that if you decline an order for a customer that the customer will take his business elsewhere. Whether you approve the orders yourself or have your staff do it, you need to balance the risk of losing the order with the risk of losing the money if your customer can't or won't pay you. The key is not using the word "No" when you're talking to the customer. Instead, offer him choices that let you ship the order within your policy.

The solution lies in understanding why the order has to be credit approved. Is it because the account is past due? Is it because the account is over the limit? Either reason comes back to your policy.

If you set up the credit limit based on the buying habits of the customer, you may hit the credit limit even when the account is current and not be prepared to increase it because you don't have enough information. If that's the case, you can ask the customer for more information to support an increased limit. Ask for financial statements or security to make the risk more acceptable. If the customer is reasonable he should help you find a way to increase his limit. If the account is past due and you want to be paid before releasing the order, you can again refer back to your procedure which states that your policy is to not ship to past due accounts. (never use the words "can't" or "won't". Instead say "policy doesn't let me" or "policy won't allow me to." Or even better "let's see what we can do to get your order approved")

If you've been managing the customer properly you should have some options available to you;

- if the account is past due, ask the customer to fax you a copy of a current dated, signed copy of a cheque. The assumption is that if the customer goes to the trouble of making out a cheque and signing it then he will mail it. Release only one order while waiting for the cheque
- don't agree to ship an order on COD terms to a customer that is past due. If you do, then your leverage is gone and the customer has no incentive to bring the account current
- if the account is over the limit ask for a cheque to bring it below the limit while you review your credit file so that you can find a way to increase the limit. Don't give in to a demand to increase the limit because the account is current. You set the limit for a reason, now you need to manage within the limit in order to control your exposure
- in either of the above cases you are demonstrating to the customer that you are trying to find a way to ship the order *within your procedure and policy*. You can blame the process for keeping you from approving the order. Ask the customer how he can help you ship him without exceeding policy. He might give you some creative ideas like paying you by credit card or giving your sales rep a cheque to get the account back below the limit

You can always ask the customer to give you some time to review his account and see if you can make an exception to the policy. He should understand that you are trying to find a way to make the sale and he should give you some time to decide. If he's demanding and threatens to take his business elsewhere you may need to let him do that. Don't put yourself at risk just to please an angry customer. If you do he'll know how to get around you next time.

If a Customer Threatens to Take His Business to a Competitor

It can be intimidating if a customer threatens to take his business elsewhere unless you increase his limit, take him off hold or let him pay you beyond terms. If that happens you need to rely on your written procedure and policy to back you up. Tell the customer that policy doesn't allow you to take him off hold or let him pay you beyond terms. It's not personal; all customers are treated the same way.

If he insists and especially if he gets angry about your decision then you can deflate the situation by telling him that you'll give his request some thought and get back to him. You may need a time out to collect your thoughts and let him cool down.

If it's the first time you've had discussions with the customer about his payments, his limit or your terms then you can defuse the situation by making a one time exception in return for a payment commitment. This lets you ship the order without compromising your policy. You can then review the file and decide on the limit without the pressure of his calls.

If however the customer has a pattern of making and breaking agreements, then you should stay with your original decision. A reasonable person will understand that you have policies that determine how you decide in situations like these. I would not allow the customer to intimidate you since if you do he will do so again and you will have shown him how to get his own way in future You may have to say something like "I understand your decision, I hope that you understand ours."

In my experience, the only customers I have lost in situations like this are the ones that end up being a problem. If the customer can't or won't work with you to find a solution, he probably has problems with other suppliers as well. In most cases, when I kept to my original decision, the customer has called me back and we've worked out a solution. In the cases when the customer took his business elsewhere the customer has turned out to have very serious financial problems and he thought he could bully me into a wrong decision.

Outsourcing Collections

If you have a large volume of customers and don't want the expense of hiring a lot of people, one alternative is to outsource the collections. There are only a couple of companies in Canada that can handle large volumes effectively. I've worked with one and can provide you with the information if you contact me directly.

Here are the critical points you will want to consider;

(i)   the process must be transparent to your customers. They can't think that you have turned the account over to a collection agency

(ii)   you should only pay for results (a contingency fee)

(iii)   the process must be more efficient than what you are doing now or you won't get value for your investment

(iv)   you will need a way of getting the invoice details and customer contact information to the outsource electronically

(v)   you will need staff who can confirm payment and pull any back up documents the customer might ask for

(vi)   you need to be able to cancel the contract with little or no penalty if it's not working out to your benefit

(vii)   the outsourcing agency must have a highly efficient phone system (usually in the form of a predictive dialer)

(viii) the customer will still remit payments to you and you still need to control the credit approval process

Beware of the "Gotta Have"

If anyone is going to cause you a bad debt loss, it's the "Gotta Have." He's the customer that places an order at the very last minute. It might be the last day of the month or the quarter end and the order might be enough for your sales staff to exceed quota and earn a bonus. That's exactly what he wants; to have sales put pressure on credit to release the order.

The "Gotta have" doesn't care about pricing and he doesn't want to hear about your procedures and policy. He wants his order and he wants it now. He'll put pressure on credit to release the order even if you have never done business with him before. He might even send you a copy of a cheque. If he's creative, it might even look like a certified cheque.

Don't walk away from this kind of order; run! No reasonable customer will place a last minute order without allowing you to determine the risk involved. The "Gotta Have" is almost always desperate to get your product so that he can sell it quickly for cash or he's a con artist that has no intention of paying you.

I've had a "Gotta Have" show up at the pickup window for an order that he placed while he was driving to our warehouse. If you know the customer well and you trust that's he's placing an honest order, go ahead and process it within your policy. If however you don't know him or his order appears too good to be true, take the time to find out why. You may not make the sale but you won't have the risk of a bad debt either.

Remember: The best friend the "Gotta Have" has may be your sales staff who want to make the sales despite the risk involved.

APPENDIX

Comprehensive Credit and Collection Procedure and Policy

New Account Application Form

Inventory Security Agreement

Collection Call Template

How to Overcome the Most Common Excuses for Non Payment

Factoring Worksheet

Proof of Claim (Bankruptcy)

Schedule "A"

New Account Letter

Statement of Account Fax

Past Due Fax

Second Request

Ten Day Demand

Small Dollar Demand

Sample in Depth Financial Analysis

How to Make a Claim in Small Claims Court (Ontario)

Plaintiff's Claim

Terms of Settlement, Small Claims Court

Demand for Repossession of Goods (30 day goods)

Comprehensive Credit and Collection Procedure and Policy

Policy

It is the responsibility of the Credit Department to review and grant credit in accordance with the Company's policy and procedures, to maximize sales while minimizing bad debts. Credit terms may only be granted and approved by the credit department.

Procedure

This procedure and policy explains in detail how the Credit Department will meet these responsibilities and add value to the Company.

New Accounts

The Credit Department will complete a credit investigation and open (or decline) all new accounts within two business day of receiving a completed, signed credit application.

Standard terms of sale are net 30 days. Customers that wish to buy product on terms must provide a completed and signed credit application. It is acceptable for the customer to sign the application and attach a list of credit references and banking information however; the credit application must be signed to ensure compliance with various privacy laws, to establish that the person signing the application is authorized to bind the company and to determine the legal name of the customer. If the customer submits an unsigned credit application, it must be returned to the customer for signature *before* any credit investigation is started.

If the customer states on the application that they are tax exempt, the customer must provide either a current tax exemption certificate or a blanket tax exemption certificate. If the tax exempt certificate is not provided, a fax or email should be sent to the customer requesting a copy. However, the credit investigation should not be delayed while waiting for the certificate to be received from the customer. If the certificate is not provided but the credit investigation has been completed, the application should be processed and the customer should be charged sales tax on all purchases until a sales tax exemption is provided. It may be necessary to refund the customer for any sales tax charged while waiting for the certificate to be received however a certificate must be provided and stored in the customer credit file at head office if the customer claims to be exempt.

Credit Requests Up To $5,000

The minimum credit limit for open, net 30 day terms is $500

The Accounts Receivable (A/R) staff is responsible for investigating all new credit applications for their respective accounts. The A/R staff is authorized to approve new limits up to $5,000 under the following guidelines;

A. Using Equifax as the reporting source

- an Equifax report must be requested for all new applications,
- if the Equifax Credit Information (CI) Score is 20 or less *and* the Payment Index (PI) is 30 or less, the A/R staff is authorized to continue as follows;

1. credit limits up to $5,000 can be established and approved by the A/R staff based on the number of years the applicant has been in business as follows;
2. for customers that have been in business for one year or less, the maximum credit approval is $500.
3. for each additional year after the first year, one thousand ($1,000) can be granted (for example, a customer in business for 2 years will have an approved limit of $1,500 ($500 + $1,000 = $1,500) to a maximum of $5,000. If the requested credit limit exceeds $5,000 then the investigation should be completed by the A/R staff then forwarded to the Credit Manager

- approved limits are based on the applicants expected 45* day purchases *or* the amount applied for on the application, whichever is *less* (*use 1.5 times the net terms)
- if there is no Equifax report available *or* if the Equifax CI score exceeds 20 *or* the PI exceeds 30, the A/R staff cannot approve open terms. The application must be referred to the Credit Manager to find a way to grant credit terms.

B. Using Dun & Bradstreet as the reporting source

- a D&B report must be requested for all new applications,
- if the Paydex score is 50 or higher and *both* the Credit Score Class *and* the Financial Stress Class are 3 or less the A/R staff is authorized to continue as follows;

1. for customers that have been in business for one year or less, the maximum credit approval is $500.
2. for each additional year after the first year, one thousand ($1,000) can be granted (for example, a customer in business for 2 years will have an approved limit of $1,500 ($500 + $1,000 = $1,500) to a maximum of $5,000
3. approved limits are based on the applicants expected 45* day purchases *or* the amount applied for on the application, whichever is *less* (use 1.5 times the net terms)
4. if there is no D&B report available *or* if the D&B Paydex Score is less than 50 *or* the Credit Score Class *or* the Financial Stress Score is more than 3, the A/R staff cannot approve open terms. The application must be referred to the Credit Manager who will follow the process outlined in paragraph C below. If the requested credit limit exceeds $5,000 then the investigation should be completed by the Credit staff then forwarded to the Credit Manager

C. For customers that do not meet the above stipulations

The Credit Manager will make every effort to find a way to grant credit terms including; contacting the applicant for additional information including financial statements, researching the applicant online and through public records and by contacting other credit grantors.

The Credit Manager will make a final determination before a credit application is refused.

If the customer does not state the maximum credit required on the application, Credit will contact the sales staff to determine the amount of credit required by the customer.

Credit Requests Between $5,000 and $25,000

The Credit Manager is authorized to approve up to $25,000 after reviewing the D&B or Equifax report provided by the A/R staff and verifying that;

- the CI is 20 or less *and* the PI is 30 or less,
- the Credit Manager must investigate any third party items or derogatory items before proceeding,
- there is satisfactory overall trade information
- trade references are checked
- financial statements may be required, depending on the limit being requested and the other available information

The Credit Manager will determine the appropriate credit limit based on the experience of other suppliers reporting to Equifax or D&B, the bank reference, the length of time in business and the background (if known) of the principals. If the Equifax or D&B report is inconclusive or not satisfactory, the Credit Manager may request that the customer provide financial statements that show adequate working capital and equity.

Credit Requests In Excess of $25,000

Financial statements are to be requested for any credit application in excess of $25,000. The Credit Manager will provide an Equifax or D&B report and an analysis of the financial statement to the Chief Financial Officer (CFO). The Credit Manager will make a recommendation to the CFO for approval. Requests in excess of $50,000 also require the approval of the President.

If the customer does not provide a financial statement, the Credit Manager will advise the customer of the company policy and try to negotiate a statement or approval to contact the customer's accountant. If the customer continues to decline the request for financial statements, the Credit Manager will provide the available information to the President and the CFO along with his recommendation. The President and the CFO may make a decision to proceed without financial information and will provide the Credit Manager with written approval to set a credit limit in excess of the policy guidelines.

Account Opening Procedure

Once the credit limit has been established and approved, the A/R staff will open the new account and send the customer a welcoming letter advising the customer of the account number and credit limit and terms. An email will be sent to the Sales Manager confirming that the account has been opened and advising the credit limit. Any notes that the A/R staff wants to pass on to the Sales Manager should be included in the email.

If open terms are declined, the customer will receive a letter and the Sales Manager must be advised by email. Customers who have been declined credit terms can purchase product on a cash basis. Cash includes Credit Card, Money Orders and Bank Drafts.

Orders Released to Customers on Hold

Orders to customers on hold may not be released under any terms, including for cash. All sales and A/R staff must bring any violations of this policy to the attention of the Credit Manger immediately. The Credit Manager will investigate and present the facts to the CFO.

Confidentiality of Information

All staff, including the credit staff will respect the customers' right to confidentiality at all times. Many customers are sole proprietors of their company or are consumers protected under various privacy acts. No detailed credit issues will be discussed with staff outside of the Credit department. Any requests for confidential information must be declined. If the requests persist, the issue must be referred to the Credit Manager.

Key Account Report

On a monthly basis, the Credit Manager will provide a report to the CFO for all past due accounts that owe $10,000 or more. The report will include the credit limit, the total balance and the aging of the account. The Credit Manager will add any comments that the CFO should be aware of, including any issues or concerns that might delay payment.

Collection of Past Due Invoices

Collection of past due invoices is one of the primary responsibilities of the Credit Department and sales staff are asked to refer customers to Credit without discussing payment specifics.

The purpose of keeping accounts current is to maximize cash flow, reduce bad debts and to keep the customer in a ready to buy position. It is the responsibility of the A/R staff to keep their respective accounts current.

On the first working day of each fiscal month, A/R staff will run an aging of their accounts. It is the A/R staff's responsibility to take the appropriate steps to bring the account current on an escalating collection basis as follows;

1. if the entire account is over 90 days old or older, the account must be put on hold and the credit limit changed to $0. Sales must be advised immediately that no new orders can be processed for the customer, even on a cash basis until the account is current and a credit investigation is completed. A statement of account must be sent to the customer either by fax or attached to an email. The fax or email must advise the customer that no orders can be processed until the account is current. A note must be entered in the customer log confirming that the statement has been sent.

    New orders can be released if the customer provides a fax copy of a cheque, payment by credit card or agrees to pay the full past due balance when picking up a new order.

2. if the entire balance is not over 90 days but there are past due invoices, a statement must be faxed or emailed to the customer along with a request to bring the account current. A copy of the statement must be filed for follow up in 14 days from the date the statement is sent to the customer. A note must be entered in the customer log confirming that the statement has been sent.

3. 14 days from the date that the statement is sent to the customer, the A/R staff must follow up to determine if the customer has made a payment to bring the account current. If the account is now current, the A/R staff can discard the copy of the statement that was filed. If the account is not current, the A/R staff can refax or email the same statement, adding "SECOND REQUEST" so that the customer is aware that this is a second request for payment. The second request copy is filed for follow up in 7 days from the date it is sent to the customer. A note must be entered in the customer log confirming that the statement has been sent.

4. if the account is not current within 7 days of the second request, a final demand must be faxed to the customer. A hold must be placed on the account and Sales must be advised that no new orders can be processed, even for cash until the account is current. A note must be entered in the customer log to confirm that the demand has been sent.

5. 10 days after the final demand date, if the account is not paid in full then a third party final demand is issued. The third party will monitor the account and follow up with the A/R staff for the status. If, after 10 days the customer has not paid the account, the collection agency will ask for permission to begin collection activity. If it becomes necessary to place an account for collection, the Credit Manager must approve the recommendation of the A/R staff. The status of the account is changed, a note is entered in the customer log and the credit limit is reset to $0. An email must be sent to Sales to advise them of our action. A note must be entered in the customer log.

Once the collection agency has begun collections, all correspondence from the customer must be directed to the collection agency. Sending statements to customers and asking for payment may result in the customers contacting the A/R staff to request invoice copies, proof of delivery and other information. Any and all contact with the customer should be noted in the customer log. If the customer brings the account current as a result of this collection activity, then the terms and limit *may* be reinstated.

Each A/R staff is responsible for keeping their respective accounts current and the aging is a key measurement of the staff's performance.

Throughout the collection process, the A/R staff must conduct themselves in a courteous and professional manner and avoid becoming emotional. Abusive, threatening or profane customers should be transferred to the Credit Manager.

Negotiating Release From Hold;

Customers can negotiate a temporary release from hold by faxing a copy of a cheque that pays the over 90 days balance to the Credit department. The release from hold is for one order only to allow for receipt of the cheque. Additional orders can not be released until the cheque is received. If the cheque is not received, the account remains on hold and the collection escalation process will continue.

Work out plans;

Only the Credit Department is authorized to arrange a workout plan with a customer.

Sometimes customers will experience cash flow problems due to no fault of their own. We value these customers and will work with them to bring the account current over a reasonable amount of time (usually 90 days or less). Customers who are experiencing cash flow problems may buy new product on a 2 for 1 basis. When the customer places a new order an agreement must be reached that the customer will pay an equal amount towards the old A/R balance. For example, if the new order is for $100 then the customer must pay $200; the additional $100 will be applied toward reducing the old balance.

If the customer is not placing new orders but agrees to pay the balance over time, a repayment plan can be negotiated with the Credit Manager. The Credit Manager will reach a reasonable repayment plan to be agreed to in writing with the customer. The customer must provide post dated cheques that cover the repayment schedule.

NSF Cheques;

NSF (Not Sufficient Funds) cheques are usually due to poor cash flow or management issues with the customer. The fact that the customers' bank won't cover the cheque, is a clear warning sign that the customer presents a higher than average risk of a loss.

If a customer provides an NSF cheque, the A/R staff must immediately put the account on hold, change the credit limit to $0 and advise the branch that no new orders can be placed, even for cash until the NSF cheque is replaced.

When a customer issues an NSF cheque, it is a clear sign that our company is at risk of not being paid for the amount of the cheque plus any other outstanding balance. If the customer indicates that they are willing to pay the balance but are having cash flow problems, the A/R staff may agree to a workout plan. However, if the customer states that they can't or won't pay the balance, the A/R staff must issue a 10 day demand covering the full amount of the balance owing, including the NSF cheque and the $25 bank fee.

Future credit terms can only be approved by the Credit Manager. Before terms can be reconsidered, the customer must replace the cheque with cash, a bank transfer of funds, or a certified cheque *and* pay an NSF fee of $25.00. The Credit Manager will request a financial statement from the customer that shows adequate working capital and equity before considering the reinstatement of terms.

Setting, Managing and Resetting Credit Limits

When credit limits for new accounts are set, the limit is based on the anticipated purchases that the customer will make in a 45 day period. If the customer exceeds the established credit limit, it is usually because the customer is buying more than originally anticipated or paying slower than 45 days. Either reason requires that the credit limit be reviewed.

It is the responsibility of the A/R staff to monitor any of their accounts that exceed the credit limit. Each Monday, the A/R staff will run an over limit report for their respective accounts and manage the credit limit as per the following guidelines;

1. if the account is current (within 45 days) and the customer has exceeded the credit limit, then the credit limit can be increased up to the total outstanding based on favourable past experience with the customer to a maximum of $3,000. If the customer requires a credit limit of more than $3,000 then an Equifax or D&B report must be requested and the credit limit reset based on the guidelines set for New Accounts. Note that credit limits over $5,000 require the Credit Manager's approval.
2. if the account is past due (over 45 days) then the credit limit should not be changed until the account is current. The A/R staff should have already started the collection process under the section "Collection of Past Due Invoices." If the collection process has not been started, it must begin based on the over limit report.
3. if the entire balance of the account is over 90 days, the account must be put on hold and the credit limit reset to $0.
4. when the A/R staff has completed the report, they must sign and date the last page of the report to confirm that they have completed the review and complied with policy. A copy of the report must be provided to the Credit Manager by the following Monday morning.

Avoidable Losses

If a customer's account is current and within the credit limit yet the Company faces a bad debt write off, that is considered an *unavoidable loss* and a risk of granting credit terms. If however, the customer is past due or over the credit limit and new orders are shipped on terms then that is an *avoidable loss*. If the A/R staff request that an account be written off to bad debt, the Credit Manager will review the open items, the past due items and the efforts that were made to collect the account. If the A/R staff did not follow proper procedure and policy and exposed the company to an avoidable loss, the Credit Manager will review the file and take remedial action to avoid a similar loss in future. A/R staff that continuously exposes the Company to avoidable losses by not following procedure and policy will be disciplined up to and including being terminated for cause.

Reserve For Doubtful Accounts

The Credit Manager will prepare a reserve for doubtful accounts on a quarterly basis and will present it to the CFO. The reserve will be set after the Credit Manager reviews all outstanding balances and makes a determination of the collectability of each account. The reserve, along with any requested write offs must be submitted to the CFO one week prior to each fiscal quarter end.

Bad Debt Write Offs

The Credit Manager is authorized to write off up to $5,000.00 on accounts that are determined to be uncollectible. Accounts in excess of that amount must be approved by the CFO and the President.

NEW ACCOUNT APPLICATION FORM

LEGAL NAME OF APPLICANT: _____

DOING BUSINESS AS: _____

STREET ADDRESS & CITY: _____

PROVINCE AND POSTAL CODE: _____

PHONE NUMBER: _____ FAX NUMBER: _____

TYPE OF BUSINESS: _____ SIZE (SQ. FT.) _____

BRANCH AND/OR SHIP TO ADDRESSES: _____

WAREHOUSING: NAME, ADDRESS AND OWNER IF DIFFERENT FROM APPLICANT:
_____
_____
_____

TYPE OF BUSINESS: (CHECK ONE)
SOLE PROPRIETOR __ PARTNERSHIP __ INCORPORATED COMPANY __

SIN# (only if not incorporated) _____ PRIMARY ADDRESS IF SOLE PROPIETORSHIP
_____

NUMBER OF YEARS IN BUSINESS IN ABOVE NAME: ( ) IF INCORPORATED, WAS BUSINESS
CONDUCTED PREVIOUSLY? YES __ NO __ IF YES, PLEASE PROVIDE DETAILS: _____
_____
_____

NAME OF BANK, BRANCH : _____ PHONE #: _____
CITY/TOWN: _____ YEARS: _____ CONTACT: _____
TAX EXEMPTION CLAIMED Y/N (ATTACH CERTIFICATE)

PLEASE PROVIDE THE NAME, ADDRESS AND PHONE/FAX # FOR 3 TRADE REFERENCES:
   1. _____
   2. _____
   3. _____

AMOUNT OF CREDIT REQUESTED, IF OPEN ACCOUNT: $_____
(FINANCIAL STATEMENT MAY BE REQUIRED)

ACCOUNTS PAYABLE CONTACT: NAME: _____
FAX #: _____ PHONE #: _____ EMAIL: _____

Please attach a void cheque to set up your account for payment through our bank lockbox

TERMS AND CONDITIONS

Applicant agrees that:

1) If accepted and granted a credit limit, they will make payment when due. Delinquency occurs immediately following the due date.

2) If a credit limit and terms are granted, they may be changed or terminated without notice at any time

3) Terms of payment will be those as stated on Seller's invoices or other documentation issued from time to time by Seller

4) Seller has the right to apply payments as they, in their sole discretion, deem appropriate

5) Interest on delinquent accounts will be charged at 18% per annum calculated monthly not in advance

6) No payment term on a purchase order will be enforceable unless acknowledged in writing by Seller

7) No oral statement by an employee of Seller will be binding on Seller, unless confirmed in writing

8) All Volume Rebates, Co-Op Advertising funds and any other benefits will be as decided by Seller in their sole discretion from time to time

9) They will be responsible for all collection and/or legal expenses if such action is deemed necessary for any reason

10) Title to goods does not transfer from the Seller to the Purchaser until invoices are paid

11) This application in its entirety shall be construed in accordance with and shall be governed by the laws of the Province of _____ and any action taken to enforce the terms and condition shall be taken in the Courts of the Province of _____ and shall be binding upon the parties hereto and their respective heirs, executors, legal personal representative, successors and assigns.

This is to certify that the foregoing information is submitted for the purpose of obtaining credit from Seller. The undersigned applicant further certifies that all information given herein is true and correct, they have the authority to bind the Company and hereby authorizes and consents to the receipt and exchange of credit information by Seller from time to time with any agency, bureau, person or corporation with whom the applicant has or purposes to have financial relations.

Signed at _____ this _____ day of _____, _____

Witness: _____   Applicant's Signature_____
                                              Business Name _____

Signature: _____
Name: _____
Address: _____
_____

Continuing Personal Guaranty

In consideration for credit extended, the undersigned contracts and agrees to be liable for all of the obligations of the Applicant to the Seller as principal obligor. The undersigned shall pay to Seller any and all obligations owing to the Seller by said Applicant as and when due by Applicant. The undersigned expressly waives all notice of acceptance of this guarantee, notice of extension or increase of credit, presentment of demand for payments, any notice of default by the company seeking credit and all other notices that the undersigned might be entitled to. Revocation of this guaranty shall be in writing and delivered by certified mail. Service on the undersigned may be made at Applicant's address shown above.

Signature_____Date_____

Address_____Phone_____

This is the second page of the credit application.

INVENTORY SECURITY AGREEMENT

Vendor (herein called the "Security Party") and

_____ (herein called the "Customer")
(Full Name of Customer)

The principal place of business of the Customer
is_____
(Street Address), (City) (Province)

HEREBY AGREE AS FOLLOWS:

1. **SCOPE OF AGREEMENT**

    The Customer is engaged in the business of buying, selling and generally dealing in new and used goods and products, including, without limitation electronic equipment. In order to enable the Customer to purchase Inventory, as defined below, the Secured Party may advance to the Customer such credit as the Secured Party in its sole discretion may deem advisable which advances are to be secured by a purchase-money security interest granted by the Customer.

2. **DEFINITIONS**

    In this Agreement, the following terms shall have the corresponding meaning as set out:

    a) "Inventory" includes all goods and products manufactured, sold, distributed or financed by Secured Party or by such others from time to time that are held by the Customer for sale or lease to the public or that are furnished under a contract of service or otherwise.

    b) "Proceeds" includes all cash and non-cash proceeds received by the Customer upon the sale or lease of Inventory including, without limitation, all accounts, contracts rights, and also chattel paper and instruments together with any amounts payable pursuant to policies of insurance covering Inventory.

    c) "Obligations" include,

        i) all amounts and advances owing or that may become owing by the Customer to the Secured Party as set out in this Agreement or any other agreement between the parties;

        ii) any other liabilities and obligations, whether monetary or otherwise, now existing or hereafter arising in favour of the Secured Party, including any solicitor's fees and expenses to which the Secured Party may be entitled as further provided in this Agreement.

3. **SECURITY INTEREST AND COLLATERAL**

    As security for the payment by the Customer of the Obligations under this Agreement, the Customer hereby grants to the Secured Party a purchase-money security interest in all of the present and hereafter acquired Inventory of the Customer and all Proceeds therefrom, which Inventory and Proceeds collectively constitute the Collateral created by this Agreement.

    The Secured Party and Customer agree that where Inventory is sold to the Customer, the property in, ownership of and title to that Inventory shall not pass to the Customer, but shall remain with the Secured Party until each item of Inventory has been paid in full to the Secured Party.

4. **WARRANTIES**

    The Customer represents and warrants to the Secured Party as follows:

    a) If the Customer is a corporation, partnership, or other business entity, that it (i) is duly incorporated (if a corporation), organized, validly existing and in good standing under the laws of the Province of _____, (ii) the name of the Customer set out herein is and always has been the legal name and that it will not change its name by amalgamation or by any other means without notifying the Secured Party in writing 10 days before so doing, (iii) is duly qualified to do business in every jurisdiction in which such qualification is necessary, (iv) has the power and authority to own its properties and to carry on its business as now being conducted and to execute and perform its obligations under this Agreement, and (v) has duly authorized the execution, delivery and performance of this Agreement;

    b) No approval is required from any regulatory body, board, authority or commission, nor from any other administrative governmental agency, nor from any other person, firm or corporation with respect to the execution of this Agreement by the Customer and the payment and performance by the Customer of all of the Customer's Obligations thereunder, or, if required, such approval has been obtained;

c) Execution, delivery and performance of this Agreement by the Customer has not and will not violate any provision of any law, court order or any provision in another agreement to which the Customer is a party or by or under which the Customer or any property of the Customer is bound, or be in conflict with, result in breach of, or constitute a default under any such agreement, or result in the creation or imposition of any lien, charge or encumbrance of any nature whatsoever upon any property or assets of the Customer;

d) No mortgage, deed of trust or other lien, charge or encumbrance of any nature whatsoever which now covers or affects, or which may hereafter cover or affect, any property or interest therein of the Customer, now attaches or hereafter will attach to the Collateral thereunder or in any manner affect or will affect adversely the Secured Party's right, title and interest herein;

e) There are no legal proceedings pending, or, to the knowledge of the Customer threatened, in any Court or before any regulatory commission, board or other administrative governmental agency against or affecting the Customer which have or will have a material adverse affect on the financial condition or business of the Customer;

f) All information concerning the financial condition and business operations of the Customer which have been or will be submitted to the Secured Party thereunder shall be true and correct in all material respects; and

g) Except for the security interest created hereby, the Customer is, or with respect to Collateral (including contractual rights with respect thereto) acquired after the date hereof, will be the owner of the Collateral, free from any mortgage, lien, charge, security interest or encumbrance of any kind whatsoever.

5.   **COVENANTS AND DUTIES**

a) The Customer will keep and maintain the Collateral only at its principal place of business and other locations set out in Schedule "A" attached and the Customer will notify the Secured Party immediately in writing of any proposed change in its place or places of business and will not remove any Collateral to a new place of business without the prior consent of the Secured Party.

b) The Customer will, from time to time, forthwith on the Secured Party's request, do, make and execute all such further assignments, documents, acts, matters and things as may be reasonably requested by the Secured Party with respect to the Collateral or any parts thereof or as may be required to give effect to the security interest granted to the Secured Party thereunder.

c) The Customer will, upon the purchase of each new or used item of Inventory, at the request of the Secured Party, deliver the certificate of title or certificate of origin, if any, issued for such items of Inventory to the Secured Party, and the Secured Party shall have the right to have its security interest noted hereon and to return in its possession the certificate of title or certificate of origin so noted.

d) The Customer will keep complete and accurate records of its business, which shall be available for the Secured Party's inspection at all reasonable times, and will furnish to the Secured Party such information regarding its business and financial condition as may be requested. The Secured Party, or its agents, may enter the premises of the Customer to perform reasonable Inventory inspections.

e) The Customer will keep the Collateral in good order and repair and will pay all taxes, assessments or charges which may be levied or assessed against the same, and in the event of failure to comply with the foregoing, any amounts expended by the Secured Party as it, in its sole discretion may deem to be necessary to repair or put the Collateral into operating condition or to pay any and all taxes, assessment and charges to be discharged, shall be considered an Obligation which is secured by this Security Agreement.

f) The Customer will at all times keep the Inventory insured for its full replacement cost against risks of fire (including extended coverage), theft, sprinkler leakage and any other risks that the Secured Party may require, with loss payable to the Secured Party and to the Customer as their respective interests may appear. All policies of insurance shall provide for 30 days written minimum cancellation notice to the Secured Party and at the request of the Secured Party shall be delivered to and held by it. Where the Customer fails to procure such insurance, The Secured Party may produce the same and the cost hereof shall be considered an Obligation under this Agreement.

g) The Customer will not sell or otherwise transfer any Collateral or interest herein other than in the ordinary course of business, and, upon any sale or transfer, the Customer agrees to hold the proceeds as trustee for the Secured Party until such time as the amounts payable by the Customer shall have been paid to the Secured Party.

h) The Customer will pay all Obligations when due as indicated on any invoices, statements or other documents submitted to the Customer from time to time and in any event will, upon the sale or other disposition of any item of Inventory out of the ordinary course of business, immediately pay the Secured Party the amount of the Customer's then outstanding Obligations allocable to the Inventory so sold.

i) The Customer will keep the Collateral (including any contractual rights in connection therewith) free and clear of all mortgages, liens, charges, security interests or other encumbrances of any kind whatsoever and shall promptly notify the Secured Party of any loss of or damage to the Collateral or any part thereof.

6. **EVENTS OF DEFAULT-ACCELERATION**

Any or all Obligations shall, at the option of the Secured Party become immediately due and payable without notice or demand upon the occurrence of any of the following events of default:

a) Default in the payment of any amount hereunder when due or in the performance of any Obligation, covenant or liability referred to herein or in any note or in any other agreement between the parties hereto evidencing the same;

b) Any warranty, representation or statement made or furnished to the Secured Party by the Customer which proves to have been false in any material respect when made or furnished in the opinion of the Secured Party attachment thereof;

c) Any event which results in the acceleration of the maturity of a debt of the Customer to others under any agreement.

d) Loss, theft, damage, destruction, sale(other than in the ordinary course of business) of any item of the Inventory or any levy, distress, seizure or attachment thereof;

e) Death (where the Customer is an individual), dissolution, termination of existence, insolvency, business failure, appointment of a receiver/manager of any part of the Customer's Collateral, assignment for the benefit of creditors, or the commencement of any proceedings under any bankruptcy or insolvency laws by or against the Customer or any guarantor of the Customer; and

f) Where the Secured Party, in good faith, believes any Collateral is or is about to be placed in jeopardy or otherwise reasonably believes any advance by it or its security interest in the Collateral to be insecure.

7. **RIGHTS AND REMEDIES ON DEFAULT**

Upon the occurrence of any such event of default, and at any time thereafter, the Customer agrees that the Secured Party shall have the rights and remedies of a Secured Party under the Personal Property Security Act in addition to the rights and remedies provided herein or in any other instrument or paper executed by the Customer.

The Customer agrees that the Secured Party may enter the premises for the purpose of taking possession of any or all of the Collateral then in the Customer's possession or the Secured Party may require the Customer to assemble the Inventory and Proceeds and make them available to both parties. The Secured Party will give the Customer reasonable notice of the time and place of any public sale thereof or of the time after which any private sale or other intended disposition thereof is to be made.

The Secured Party may alternatively appoint by instrument any person or persons to be a receiver and manager (hereafter called "Receiver") of the Inventory and Proceeds. Any such Receiver shall have all the powers of the Secured Party set out herein as well as the power to take possession of the Inventory and Proceeds and to sell and concur in selling any such Inventory as indicated above. The Receiver shall be deemed to be the agent of the Customer in the operation of the business.

The Customer agrees to pay all expenses incurred by the Secured Party in the enforcement of any of the Obligations after default or otherwise in connection of pursuing its rights as a secured party including the expenses related to taking of possession, custody, preservation and disposition of the Collateral and legal expenses as between a solicitor and his/her own client all of which shall be secured hereunder.

In the event that the date any Inventory returned is beyond 150 days from date of original invoice and/or out of the original factory sealed carton, the value of such inventory shall be the best available commercially reasonable market price after giving consideration to missing accessories, damage and age of product. There shall be no allowance given for trade-in inventory.

The Customer shall remain liable to the Secured Party for any deficiency remaining under this Agreement after the application of the proceeds of disposition of the Collateral.

8. **POWER OF ATTORNEY**

The Customer hereby irrevocably makes, constitutes and appoints the Secured Party or any of its employees as the Customer's lawful attorney-in-fact with the power of substitution, to execute and deliver in the name of the Customer chattel mortgages or other security agreements; to cause the same to be properly transferred in the appropriate office of any jurisdiction for the registration and transfer of certificate of title or the filing or recording of financing statements, chattel mortgages or other security agreements; to mark satisfied any and all encumbrances thereon; to endorse the Customer's name upon any notes, cheques, drafts, money orders and other forms of instruments made payable to the Customer and generally to do and perform all acts and all things necessary in discharge of the power granted under this Agreement which shall specifically include the making of any acknowledgements and affidavits necessary for filing or recording of any or all of the foregoing; to make, execute and deliver in the name of the Customer, as maker, any promissory note evidencing the obligation of the Customer to pay all advances theretofore made to or on behalf of the Customer by the Secured Party constituting Obligations.

The powers granted under this Power of Attorney are understood to be coupled with an interest and shall be considered irrevocable without the prior written consent of the Secured Party for such time as any Obligations may remain outstanding.

PAID

9.   GENERAL

It is further agreed as follows:

a)   The Secured Party shall not be deemed to have waived any of the Secured Party's rights hereunder or under any other agreement, instrument or paper signed by the Customer unless such waiver be in writing and signed by the Secured Party. No delay or omission on the part of the Secured Party in exercising any right shall operate as a waiver of such right or remedy on any future occasion. All the Secured Party's rights and remedies, whether evidenced hereby or by any other agreement, instrument or paper, shall be cumulative and may be exercised singularly or concurrently. This Agreement and all rights and obligations hereunder including matters of constructions, validity and performance, shall be governed by the laws of the Province of _____. This Agreement is intended to take effect and attach when signed by the Customer and delivered to the Secured Party.

b)   Any document evidencing the sale to the Customer of Inventory by any vendor shall be conclusively deemed to be an invoice notwithstanding that it may be designated as a conditional sale contract or otherwise described and such document shall not constitute a security agreement.

c)   This Agreement may not be modified, altered or amended except by a further agreement in writing signed by the parties hereto.

d)   Any provision of this Agreement found upon judicial interpretation or construction to be prohibited by law shall not invalidate the remaining provisions hereof.

e)   If more than one person execute this Agreement their obligations hereunder shall be joint and several.

f)   Where the Customer is, in law or in fact, a partnership, the Agreement is binding upon that partnership and upon each partner in that partnership jointly and severally as if each such partner had executed this Agreement and assumed all of the rights, duties and obligations of the Customer herein.

g)   This Agreement and the rights and obligations of the Customer hereunder are not assignable, in whole or in part, without the written consent of the Secured Party. It is agreed that the Secured Party may assign this Agreement and the rights and obligations hereunder, in whole or in part, at any time and from time to time.

h)   This Agreement shall enure to the benefit of and bind the Customer and the Secured Party and their respective heirs, executors, legal personal representatives, successors and assigns.

i)   The Customer acknowledges receipt of a copy of this Security Agreement.

j)   If the Customer is a corporation, it agrees that the provisions of the Conditional Sales Act in the Province of Alberta, the provisions of the Sale of Goods on Condition Act in the Province of British Columbia and the provisions of the Limitation of Civil Rights Act in the Province of Saskatchewan shall have no application to the terms of this Security Agreement or have any affect on the rights, duties and obligations of the parties hereto and any such rights, benefits or protection thereunder are specifically waived by the Customer.

IN WITNESS WHEREOF, the Customer and the Secured Party have executed this Security Agreement this _____ day of
_____ _____.

Witness (Sign) _____

Name _____
        (Print)
Address _____

_____

Name of Customer in Full _____

By: _____
    (I have the authority to bind the Company)
Title: _____

By: _____
Title: _____

Vendor

By: _____
Authorized Signing Officer

91

Collection Call Template	
Date:	Follow Up Date:
Phone #:	Fax #:
Customer Name:	Account #:
Who am I speaking to?:	Amount $:

Commitment Section
How much are you sending / did you send me?
When are you sending / did you send it?
How are you sending / did you send it?

Important! If a payment has already been sent ask for a cheque number

Resolution Section

Why are you not sending payment (or partial payment)?	Index #
Need Invoice Copy	☐ A
Need Proof of Delivery	☐ B
Pricing Error	☐ C
Did Not Order	☐ D
Short Shipped or Damaged on Receipt	☐ E
Payment Has Not Been Approved	☐ F
Disagree With The Balance Owing	☐ G
I Need a Statement of Account	☐ H
Cheque Is Ready But Not Signed	☐ I
Other	☐ J

Notes:

Guide to collection template Index
How to Overcome the Most Common Excuses for Non payment
(Ian's Big Black Book)

Customers usually fall into one of the three following types;

- the Customer who buys your products and services and usually pays you more or less on time. You want to have as many of these customers in your A/R as possible. You also want your sales staff to work on building business with these Customers.
- the Customer who will eventually pay you; just not right now. You need to identify these customers as soon as possible and resolve any excuses they have for not paying you on time.
- the Customer who can't or won't pay you. These customers need to be identified immediately and you need to be aggressive in following up. As soon as the Customer tells you he can't or won't pay you, make sure the problem doesn't get worse by allowing him to buy more product or service on credit terms. Be very firm in giving the customer a date by which he must pay you and if he doesn't pay you by then, turn the account over to a third party.

Although it's not possible to cover all of the reasons that a customer gives for not paying an invoice, the following Index will give you a good response to most situations and also some guidance on how to keep the problem from happening again.

If you use this template for your collection calls and follow up on the days I recommend, you will see a significant improvement in your aging, your cash flow and your profits.

Remember; get a specific commitment from a specific person to pay you a specific amount on a specific day then follow up to make sure the commitment is kept.

Index A

Need An Invoice Copy

Recommended Reply:

"I'll fax you (or email you) a copy to-day but please understand that our terms are based on the date of the original invoice, not on the date that you receive the replacement copy."

Comments:

Asking for replacement copies of invoices is one of the most common excuses for not paying on time. Unless you can prove that the customer received the original, you probably have no choice but to provide a replacement copy. Before you do, ask the customer to verify that you are sending the originals to the right address for payment. Sometimes, product is shipped to a different address than the invoice. If the invoice went to the right address, you can advise the customer that it was sent correctly and then add that you are sending a replacement copy as a courtesy. However, the customer must understand that the terms are based on the original invoice date and not on the date the replacement copy is received. Try to avoid mailing the replacement copy since that will further delay payment. Send the copy by fax or email to avoid further delays.

To solve this problem in future, make sure the invoices are going to the right address and keep track of how often the same customer claims not to have received the original invoice. If it seems that the original is getting lost quite often, that might be a sign that the customer has a cash flow problem and that Accounts Payable is trying to slow down payments. If you suspect this is the case, try sending the original invoices by courier, fax or email. The salesman may also be able to help out by delivering the invoices in person which will give him another reason to call on the customer.

When you fax or email the original invoice or a replacement copy, attach a copy of the email or fax confirmation to the notes print out for follow up.

Index B

Need Proof of Delivery

Recommended Reply:

"I'll provide you with proof of delivery but please understand that our terms are based on the original delivery date, not on the date that you receive the Proof of Delivery."

Comments:

Asking for proof of delivery (POD) can be a common excuse to delay payment or it can be a genuine request for proof that the product was delivered. A lot depends on how long the customer took to ask for the POD. If he waited until you started calling for payment, it's probably a delaying tactic. After all, the customer issued a purchase order and received the invoice. Why did he not match up the invoice with his receiving and realize that he was short shipped or didn't get the product?

You probably have no choice but to provide a replacement copy but make sure you can prove when the copy was sent. Use either a fax or email which will then give you confirmation. Keep track of how often the customer makes the same request. If he asks for a lot of POD, then he may have a receiving problem or a cash flow problem, both of which should concern you. If he requests a lot of POD but you still want to keep shipping to him, try sending the POD immediately after the shipment is delivered. That way, he can't wait until after the invoice is due.

Another approach is to have someone (maybe the salesman) call the customer right after delivery and ask the customer to confirm that they got the product or service as agreed. Then, if someone calls asking for POD, you can refer them to the call you made when the product was delivered and tell them that delivery was confirmed.

When you fax or email the POD, attach a copy of the email or fax confirmation to the notes print out for follow up.

Index C

Pricing Error

Recommended Reply:

"When did you discover that the price on the invoice is wrong? Is the price different than the price on your purchase order? If so, I'll pull copies of both and confirm."

Comments:

Disputing prices is a common delaying tactic and can often cause problems for Accounts Receivable unless you keep copies of the customer's purchase orders. If you do keep copies, then it should be easy to compare your invoice to the original purchase order. If there is a difference you will need to investigate why. If the customer waited until your collection call before deciding that the invoice has the wrong price it may be an indication that he is trying to delay payment.

If you find that the price on the purchase order is the same as on the invoice, then provide the customer with a copy of both and remind him that the terms started with the invoice date and not the date that you sent the copies. Either fax or email the copies so that you have a record of when the copy was sent. Use this confirmation as your follow up.

If you find that the customer is correct and that your invoice has the wrong price, you can negotiate for the customer to pay the invoice at the correct price and then provide a credit note at a later date, or you can issue a credit note and either fax it or email it to the customer. Although your invoice had the wrong price, advise the customer that the terms on the original invoice determine when the invoice is due, not the date he receives the credit note. The customer may argue that he can't pay an invoice that has the wrong price on it, but you can argue that the receipt of the product or service determines when payment is due. If the customer caught the error as soon as he received the invoice, you probably haven't lost much time. However, if the customer waited until you called for payment, then you can insist on payment. It is the buyer's responsibility to check the invoice price against the purchase order price.

When you fax or email the credit note, attach a copy of the email or fax confirmation to the notes print out for follow up.

Index D

Did Not Order

Recommended Reply:

"When did you find out that we invoiced you for something that you did not order? Do you have the product? (Or, do you agree that we provided the service?) Is the purchase order on the invoice one of yours?"

Comments:

Claiming not to have ordered the product or service is a common delay tactic. If you can provide the customer with a copy of his purchase order and it agrees with the invoice, make sure the customer understands that the terms are based on the invoice date, not the date you provide a copy of the purchase order.

Sometimes the buyer does not provide accounts payable with a copy of the purchase order. That's the reason for asking if the purchase order is one of theirs. A/P may not be able to match the purchase order on the invoice to their receiving records. If you provide a copy, ask the buyer to make sure his A/P staff gets a copy of the purchase order.

If you don't keep copies of purchase orders, then you may have to provide proof of delivery to the customer. If you delivered the goods or services, then the customer may agree to pay for them even if he did not order them. If the customer insists that he did not order the product and does not want to keep it, you may have to accept a return and issue a credit note.

If the purchase order does not agree with the invoice and you can't provide proof of delivery, you may have to issue a credit note. If this happens, you need to look at your internal processes to make sure it does not happen again.

When you fax or email the purchase order or proof of delivery, attach a copy of the email or fax confirmation to the notes print out for follow up.

Index E

Short Shipped or Damaged

Recommended Reply:

"When did you discover that the shipment was short shipped or damaged? Do you have a copy of the proof of delivery where you signed for the shortage or damage? Have you contacted the carrier?"

Short shipments and damaged shipments are a part of life when shipping product to a customer. The key to resolving the problem is providing proof to the carrier as soon as possible so that you can file a claim. All carriers have a maximum time for you to file a claim. Ask the customer to fax or email you his copy of the bill of lading and the packing slip.

Ask the customer if he has already contacted the carrier and if he has, did he receive a claim number? How the product was shipped will determine who is responsible for filing a claim against the carrier. If the shipper made the arrangements for delivery, then the shipper is responsible. If the customer arranged shipment or picked up the product, then the customer is responsible. If the product was shipped Free On Board (FOB) the shipper's warehouse, then the shipper is responsible. The easiest way to determine who is responsible is to find out who paid the delivery bill.

When you receive the copy of the bill of lading or packing slip from the customer, check the signature. If the customer did sign for a shortage or damage, then file a claim with the carrier immediately. Carriers have a time limit but will usually give a few extra days if you file as soon as you find out. If the bill of lading and packing slip are signed without notice of damage or shortage, you need to advise the customer that you expect payment in full on the due date of the invoice since you can't file a claim.

If you file a claim, ask the customer to pay you the balance of the invoice so that you don't have to wait for the carrier claim to be resolved. Most customers will deduct the amount of the shortage or damage from the invoice and pay you the balance.

If it seems that the customer is waiting until the invoice is past due before he claims a shortage or damage you should remind him that there is a filing deadline for all claims and that the balance of the order is due and payable whether he has a claim or not.

Index F

Payment Not Approved

Recommended Reply:

"What needs to happen to get approval and who do I need to talk to so that payment is approved?"

Since the invoice is already past due, you want to resolve any roadblocks that are preventing you from getting paid. You need to find out where the delay is and who can resolve the delay.

All customers have a process that they must follow in order to approve an invoice for payment. Since your invoice is past due, some part of that process is not working. You provided the product or service that was ordered by the customer and your terms were part of the agreement. Ask who is holding up payment and why. Then, contact that person and remind them of the invoice terms and that you expect payment. Don't be afraid to ask for your money. The supplier that follows up will get paid first regardless of what the problem is.

Watch for warning signs;

- if accounts payable has approved payment but the signing officer has not signed your cheque that could be because of cash flow issues. Ask how long the signature will take and if you can pick up the cheque or have it sent to you by courier
- if the buyer has not approved payment, you need to find out why; after all it was the buyer who ordered your product or service.
- If the A/P staff gives you the impression that no suppliers are being paid, then you need to alert your management immediately.

Index G

Disagree With The Balance Owing

Recommended Reply:

"Why do you think the balance owing is wrong and when did you find out it was wrong?"

Sometimes you will invoice the customer incorrectly. The sooner you find out, the quicker you can solve the problem. Hopefully the customer didn't wait until the invoice was past due before he pointed out the error.

Check the invoice amount against the customer's purchase order to find out if he is correct. If not, fax or email him a copy of his purchase order to show him that you invoiced the correct amount and ask for payment based on the due date of the invoice.

If the customer is correct, he might be willing to send you the amount he agrees that he owes you. Try not to let the customer wait until he receives your credit note. If you can get a payment while you are processing the credit note, that will improve your cash flow.

If you find that you are issuing a lot of credit notes, you need to look at your internal processes to find out why. Invoicing customers incorrectly will significantly delay your collections.

If the customer consistently delays payment due to disputes that are incorrect, then he may be delaying payments. Keep track of how often the same customer complains about wrong pricing when your invoices are correct.

Index H

Need A Statement of Account

Recommended Reply:

"Our terms are based on the invoice date, not the statement date. We send you a statement as a matter of courtesy, but you need to pay based on the invoice, not the statement."

Most suppliers invoice customers throughout the month as shipments take place. Statements are usually sent at the end of a month as a courtesy to the customer, not as the primary method of invoicing.

Unless your terms are based on a statement being received by the customer, you need to advise the customer not to delay payment until he receives a statement. If he is allowed to wait until the statement is received, you are providing him with an interest free loan of your money.

Some customers will insist that you send them a monthly statement so that they can confirm that they have been invoiced correctly. This is usually an excuse since they check invoices against purchase orders, not statements. If your customer won't pay you without a statement, then fax or email the statement instead of mailing it. Remind the customer that the payment terms are based on the invoice date, not the statement date.

Customers will sometimes tell you that they need the statement to make sure they haven't been double invoiced, but again that's an excuse since A/P matches invoices, not statements.

If the customer disputes the balance on a statement or a specific invoice or credit note, ask them to pay the amount they agree that they owe while you investigate the dispute. Don't allow the customer to delay payment entirely.

Index I

Cheque Ready But Not Signed

Recommended Reply:

"If payment has been approved, we don't need a cheque. I'll give you our banking information and you can have a direct deposit made to our bank."

Depending on how large your customer is, there may be only one person to sign cheques and if that person is not available for some reason then if you may have to wait unless you're creative.

Although most payments are made by cheque, there is no reason that your customer can't deposit the money directly to your bank account. The customer's bank can make a bank to bank payment without the customer even having to go to the bank. Bank transfers are becoming more and more common and transfers have the added advantage of not being returned as NSF.

Although a physical cheque needs a signature, a bank transfer does not. Usually the bank has an agreement in place that allows your customers' staff to transfer money electronically. There may be a maximum amount that can be transferred without a signature and you may have to accept less than full payment, but don't let a lack of a signature keep you from getting at least some of your money.

Your customer will only feel embarrassed if the funds are not in the bank and you have taken away the excuse of the cheque not being signed.

Remember, if the customer wants to continue to receive your products and services, you need to be paid for what is already owing.

Once the customer makes the transfer, the funds should be in your bank account the same day or the next day at the latest.

Index J

Other

Although it's not possible to cover every single reason for not paying in this guide, you should have a better understanding of how to overcome most excuses. If you are persistent and follow up regularly you will get paid; usually before other suppliers, even if the customer has cash flow problems.

Make friends with the person in Accounts Payable who pays your account. They will sometimes bend the rules for you or give you inside information on how to get paid sooner. The A/P staff might even give you advance warning of financial problems. If your A/P contact changes often then that could be a sign of problems within your customer. Some customers change staff around just to delay payments to suppliers. If the way the A/P staff interacts with you changes suddenly, that could indicate that they are under a lot of pressure to delay payments to suppliers.

If someone makes a payment commitment to you, make sure they keep their promise by following up. They will learn that you are not a person they can put off with excuses and delays.

Keep careful notes and review your notes before you call the customer.

Use the guide and the recommended follow up process. I've learned what works best after many, many years of collecting money.

Factoring Worksheet

(A) Based on the information provided, can factoring benefit your business?
Please read below to see how factoring can work for your business.

(B) You could save the following in trade discounts by using factoring.	$1500
(C) By increasing production and sales, your additional gross profit would be.	$2040
(D) You would save the following by eliminating your current financing cost:	$623
(E) Factoring would provide you with a gross profit increase of:	$4163
(F) Estimated cost of factoring (an average flat factoring fee of 1.5% and an annualized pricing of Prime plus 1% where Prime is assumed to be at 4%).	$2400
(G) Factoring would provide a net incremental pre-tax profit of:	$1763
(H) Your profit could increase by this amount (as a percent of sales):	0.01 %
(I) The average days outstanding for your receivables is:	46 days
(J) Time it takes you to get paid after receiving an order:	46 days
(K) By receiving cash the day you ship, you improve your cash flow cycle by:	100 %

The above example is for a company with annual sales of $120,000 at 20% profit margins with terms of 1.5%, net 30 days and average days outstanding of 45 days. Your results will probably be different but it helps illustrate the value of factoring.

Form 31

Proof of Claim

Section 50.1, subsections 65.2(4), 81.2(1), 81.3(8), 81.4(8), 102(2), 124(2), 128(1), and paragraphs 51(1)(e) and 66.14(b) of the Act)

All notices or correspondence regarding this claim must be forwarded to the following address: _____

In the matter of the bankruptcy (or the proposal, or the receivership) of _____ (name of debtor) of _____ (city and province) and the claim of _____, creditor.

I, _____(name of creditor or representative of the creditor), of _____ (city and province), do hereby certify:

1. That I am a creditor of the above-named debtor (or that I am _____ (state position or title) of _____ (name of creditor or representative of the creditor)).

2. That I have knowledge of all the circumstances connected with the claim referred to below.

3. That the debtor was, at the date of bankruptcy (or the date of the receivership, or in the case of a proposal, the date of the notice of intention or of the proposal, if no notice of intention was filed), namely the _____ day of _____, ____, and still is, indebted to the creditor in the sum of $_____, as specified in the statement of account (or affidavit) attached and marked Schedule "A", after deducting any counterclaims to which the debtor is entitled. (The attached statement of account or affidavit must specify the vouchers or other evidence in support of the claim.)

4. *(Check and complete appropriate category.)*

☐   A. UNSECURED CLAIM OF $_____

(other than as a customer contemplated by Section 262 of the Act)

That in respect of this debt, I do not hold any assets of the debtor as security and

(Check appropriate description)

☐   Regarding the amount of $_____, I claim a right to a priority under section 136   of the Act.

☐   Regarding the amount of $_____ , I do not claim a right to a priority.

(Set out on an attached sheet details to support priority claim.)

☐   B. CLAIM OF LESSOR FOR DISCLAIMER OF A LEASE $_____

That I hereby make a claim under subsection 65.2(4) of the Act, particulars of which are as follows:

(Give full particulars of the claim, including the calculations upon which the claim is based.)

☐   C. SECURED CLAIM OF $_____

That in respect of this debt, I hold assets of the debtor valued at $_____ as security, particulars of which are as follows:

(Give full particulars of the security, including the date on which the security was given and the value at which you assess the security, and attach a copy of the security documents.)

☐   D. CLAIM BY FARMER, FISHERMAN OR AQUACULTURIST OF $_____

That I hereby make a claim under subsection 81.2(1) of the Act for the unpaid amount of $_____

(Attach a copy of sales agreement and delivery receipts.)

☐   E. CLAIM BY WAGE EARNER OF $_____

☐   That I hereby make a claim under subsection 81.3(8) of the Act in the amount of $_____

☐   That I hereby make a claim under subsection 81.4(8) of the Act in the amount of $_____

☐   F. CLAIM AGAINST DIRECTOR $_____

(To be completed when a proposal provides for the compromise of claims against directors.)

That I hereby make a claim under subsection 50(13) of the Act, particulars of which are as follows:

(Give full particulars of the claim, including the calculations upon which the claim is based.)

☐   G. CLAIM OF A CUSTOMER OF A BANKRUPT SECURITIES FIRM $_____

That I hereby make a claim as a customer for net equity as contemplated by section 262 of the Act, particulars of which are as follows:

(Give full particulars of the claim, including the calculations upon which the claim is based.)

5. That, to the best of my knowledge, I am (or the above-named creditor is) (or am not or is not) related to the debtor within the meaning of section 4 of the Act, and have (*or* has) (*or* have not *or* has not) dealt with the debt or in a non-arm's length manner.

6. That the following are the payments that I have received from, and the credits that I have allowed to, and the transfers at undervalue within the meaning of subsection 2(1) of the Act that I have been privy to or a party to with the debtor within the three months (or, if the creditor and the debtor are related within the meaning of section 4 of the Act, within the 12 months) immediately before the date of the initial bankruptcy event within the meaning of Section 2 of the Act: (*Provide details of payments, credits and transfers at undervalue.*)

(*Applicable only in the case of the bankruptcy of an individual.*)

☐   I request that a copy of the report filed by the trustee regarding the bankrupt's application for discharge pursuant to subsection 170(1) of the Act be sent to the above address.

Dated at _____ , this _____ day of _____ .

(signature of individual completing this form)   (signature of witness)

(creditors phone number)   (creditors fax number)

GENERAL PROXY (with Power of Substitution)

WHERE A CREDITOR IS A CORPORATION, THE PROXY MUST BE COMPLETED AND SIGNED IN THE CORPORATE NAME

IN THE MATTER OF THE BANKRUPTCY/PROPOSAL/RECEIVERSHIP OF _____

I, _____ of the City of _____ in the Province of _____

A creditor in the above matter, hereby appoint _____ of _____

To be my general proxy in the above matter except as to the receipt of dividends with/without power to appoint another general proxy in his/her place

Dated at the City of _____ , in the Province of _____ this _____ day of _____

Corporate name _____   Signature of Witness _____

Address _____   Signature of proxy grantor _____

This is Schedule "A"
Attached to the claim of Onsite Credit Group
For Goods Sold and Delivered
In the Bankruptcy of Bankrupt Customer Inc.

Invoice #12345	June 1, 2010	$100.00
Invoice #12346	June 2, 2010	$100.00
Invoice #12347	June 10, 2010	$125.00
		$325.00

Signed By:

Dated:

Be sure to attach a schedule "A" to your proof of claim. It can be in the form of a spreadsheet or a simple Word document but you must state why the bankrupt owes you the balance you are claiming. I have seen many claims disallowed simply because the debtor forgot to add "For Goods Sold and Delivered."

Ian Fearon CCE, CCP

CUSTOMER NAME
ADDRESS
CITY, PROVINCE
POSTAL CODE

Via Fax:

Attention:

Date:

Dear, **CUSTOMER NAME w**e are pleased to advise you that your request for credit terms has been approved. Your credit limit is $_____ and your terms are _____. Your account number is _____

I will be the primary contact for your accounts payable staff. My direct telephone number is _____ My email address is _____. We are looking forward to growing our business together.

Sincerely,

Ian Fearon
Credit Manager

NEW ACCOUNT WELCOME LETTER

Use this to inform new customers of the terms of sale and their credit limit. It also tells the customer who to call if they have any concerns. In case of a dispute about terms or the credit limit you can refer to this letter.

CUSTOMER NAME
ADDRESS
CITY, PROVINCE
POSTAL CODE

Via Fax:

Date:

Please find attached a copy of your statement of account as of to-day.

Kindly forward payment to bring the account current at your earliest convenience. If you have any issues or concerns you may reach me directly at 416-948-9582 or at ian@onsitecreditgroup. com

Sincerely,

Ian Fearon
Credit Manager

FAX WITH STATEMENT ATTACHED

Use this letter as a friendly reminder that there is a balance due.

Ian Fearon CCE, CCP

CUSTOMER NAME
ADDRESS
CITY, PROVINCE
POSTAL CODE

Via Fax:

Date:

Please find attached copies of our invoices #_____, #_____ and #_____ which remain outstanding. If you have not already done so, please remit payment at your earliest convenience and no later than (fax date plus 10 day).

Kindly forward payment to bring the account current at your earliest convenience. If you have any issues or concerns you may reach me directly at 416-948-9582. or at ian@onsitecreditgroup. com

Sincerely,

Ian Fearon
Credit Manager

COPY OF PASTDUE FAX

Use this as a reminder to the customer that there are specific invoices that are past due. Giving the customer 10 days to send payment reinforces that you want to be paid by a specific date.

CUSTOMER NAME
ADDRESS
CITY, PROVINCE
POSTAL CODE

Via Fax:

Date:

SECOND REQUEST

Please find attached copies of our invoices #_____, #_____ and #_____ which remain outstanding. If you have not already done so, please remit payment at your earliest convenience and no later than (*fax date plus 10 days*).

Kindly forward payment to bring the account current at your earliest convenience. If you have any issues or concerns you may reach me directly at 416-948-9582 or at ian@onsitecreditgroup.com

Sincerely,

Ian Fearon
Credit Manager

COPY OF PAST DUE FAX, SECOND REQUEST

Use this as a follow up to the above letter. You don't have to reprint the letter, just add "Second Request" to save yourself time. Then follow up on the due date.

Ian Fearon CCE, CCP

CUSTOMER NAME
ADDRESS
CITY, PROVINCE
POSTAL CODE

Via Fax:

Date:

Attention: Accounts Payable

Please find attached a copy of your statement as of this morning. As you can see, the account is considerably past due. Regretfully, we are unable to release new orders until the account is current. Please remit payment at your earliest convenience and no later than June 27.

If you have any issues or concerns you may reach me directly at 416-948-9582 or at ian@onsitecreditgroup.com

Sincerely,

Ian Fearon
Credit Manager

COPY OF ACCOUNT ON HOLD LETTER

Use this as a way to advise your customer that new orders are on hold based on the aging. Notice that it gives the customer a due date by which the payment must be received. If the customer contacts you and arranges a payment, one new order can be released while you are waiting for the payment.

CUSTOMER NAME
ADDRESS
CITY, PROVINCE
POSTAL CODE

Via Fax:

Date:

WITHOUT PREJUDICE

The purpose of this fax is to advise you that if the full balance of your account, $xx,xxx is not received in our offices by (*10 days from date of fax*), we will have no alternative but to place your account for collection.

Our agents will be instructed to collect the full balance along with costs and interest. As a member of Equifax, we report all of our collection accounts to all other members.

Please govern yourself accordingly.

Sincerely,

Ian Fearon
Credit Manager

SAMPLE 10 DAY DEMAND LETTER

Use this to demand payment by a certain date or you will place the account for collection. Telling the customer that you will also add costs and interest adds to the sense of urgency. If the customer disputes the costs and interest penalties, refer them to your credit application. Even if you're not a member of Equifax or have no intention of reporting the customer, leave the statement in your letter. Customers aren't afraid of collection letters but they know the value of their credit report.

Important; once you send this demand, you have to be prepared to place the account for collection on the 11th day. If not, the customer will not take you seriously.

Ian Fearon CCE, CCP

CUSTOMER NAME
ADDRESS
CITY, PROVINCE
POSTAL CODE

Date:

Without Prejudice

Please find attached a copy of our invoice #_____. Although we have sent copies and requested payment, our account remains unpaid.

The purpose of this fax is to advise you that if the invoice is not paid by (*10 days from the date of this letter*), we will place the account for collection. Our account will be reported to all three credit reporting agencies. I'm sure you will agree that it makes no sense to impact your credit rating with such a small amount however, we do require payment.

Please provide payment so that we do not have to report your delinquency to your other suppliers.

Sincerely,

SMALL DOLLAR 10 DAY DEMAND LETTER

Most collection agents won't accept claims under $150-$200. This demand letter tells the customer that you won't give up even though the amount is low. If the customer is concerned about his credit reputation, he will pay you. If you don't get paid within 10 days you probably have to write the balance off but this letter has proven effective in about 50% of the cases where I've used it.

The following two pages provide a sample of the in depth financial analysis that Onsite provides to our clients. The subject of our analysis is a publicly traded Canadian company

When we ran the analysis, there were several key areas of concern;

- between December 31, 2008 and March 31, 2009 the company went through more than $11 million in cash
- as of March 31, 2009 the company had a $108 million working capital deficit meaning it could not meet its debts in the ordinary course of business
- current bank debt increased from $0 to $39 Million in 3 months
- the long term debt of $82 Million as at December 31, 2008 was converted to current debt because the company had violated the terms and conditions of the bank loan
- his is a retail company that sells on a private label credit card basis. It then sells the debt at a discount. Normally the company got its cash in 15-20 days from the finance company but in late 2008 the finance company stopped providing funding so the average payment increased to 73.67 days, significantly impacting cash flow
- the company's auditors forced it to write down more than $400 Million in goodwill based on the North American recession. As a result, the company was essentially insolvent
- the Onsite insolvency prediction score of 1.40 in December 2007 turned into a -0.10 score in December 2008 and a -1.33 score in March 2009. A negative prediction score indicates that a company has a high risk of failure within 12-18 months unless significant financial changes are made
- for the full year ended December 2009 the company lost $163 Million
- the company issued debentures to an asset-based credit facility with interest rates as high as 15%
- during 2009 the company admitted to its shareholders that there was a risk to its ability to continue as a going concern
- many large suppliers demanded letters of credit (see my comments under setting credit limits) in order to keep shipping
- the company was restructured in the fourth quarter of 2009
- as of mid 2011 the company continues in business but continues to be technically insolvent
- in a highly competitive economy, we're not sure that the company can compete when it pays 12-15% interest on its debt
- a large part of the company's assets and future profits rely on suppliers continuing to provide product

	March 31 2009	% of Total	December 31, 2008	% of Total	December 31, 2007	% of Total
ASSETS						
Current						
Cash	$3,337,000	1%	$14,419,000	2%	$8,174,000	1%
Accounts Receivable	$54,816,000	9%	$69,616,000	10%	$72,757,000	8%
Income Taxes	$0	0%	$0	0%	$0	0%
Inventory	$159,059,000	26%	$207,627,000	29%	$236,703,000	24%
Prepaids & Deposits	$3,413,000	1%	$4,367,000	1%	$4,472,000	0%
Future Income Tax Assets	$0	0%	$0	0%	$0	0%
Total Current Assets	$220,625,000	37%	$296,029,000	42%	$322,106,000	33%
Marketable Securities	$20,360,000	3%	$18,912,000	3%	$24,125,000	2%
Leasehold Improvements	$1,128,000	0%	$517,000	0%	$0	0%
Deferred Acquisition Costs	$25,510,000	4%	$25,382,000	4%	$21,944,000	2%
Goodwill	$108,459,000	18%	$108,459,000	15%	$305,349,000	32%
Other Intangible Assets	$80,253,000	13%	$108,958,000	15%	$160,109,000	17%
Capital Assets	$145,733,000	24%	$146,234,000	21%	$132,766,000	14%
Other Assets	$41,000	0%	$48,000	0%	$50,000	0%
TOTAL ASSETS	$602,109,000	100%	$704,539,000	100%	$966,449,000	100%
LIABILITIES						
Current						
Bank Debt	$39,010,000	6%	$0	0%	$14,637,000	2%
Accounts Payable and accrued	$161,631,000	27%	$251,008,000	36%	$224,042,000	23%
Customer Deposits	$43,930,000	7%	$53,401,000	8%	$68,862,000	7%
Current portion of LTD	$81,503,000	14%	$0	0%	$0	0%
Income taxes payable	$0	0%	$0	0%	$81,000	0%
Other current liabilities	$2,736,000	0%	$3,099,000	0%	$2,453,000	0%
TOTAL CURRENT LIABILITIES	$328,810,000	55%	$307,508,000	44%	$310,075,000	32%
Long Term Debt	$0	0%	$82,122,000	12%	$81,955,000	8%
Deferred/Unearned Revenue	$157,093,000	26%	$155,188,000	22%	$141,832,000	15%
Future Income Taxes	$13,572,000	2%	$20,741,000	3%	$31,768,000	3%
Other Long Term Liabilities	$0	0%	$0	0%	$0	0%
Total Long Tern Liabilities	$170,665,000	28%	$258,051,000	37%	$255,555,000	26%
SHAREHOLDERS EQUITY						
Paid in Capital	$528,213,000	88%	$528,213,000	75%	$528,213,000	55%
Retained Earnings	($425,579,000)	-71%	($389,233,000)	-55%	($127,394,000)	-13%
Total Equity	$102,634,000	17%	$138,980,000	20%	$400,819,000	41%
TOTAL LIABILITIES	$602,109,000	100%	$704,539,000	100%	$966,449,000	100%

SALES	$271,599,000		$1,427,113,000		$1,447,576,000	
Cost of Sales	$161,587,000		$846,577,000		$866,377,000	
Gross Margin	$110,012,000	41%	$580,536,000	41%	$581,199,000	40%
SG&A	$112,485,000	41%	$511,473,000	36%	$504,605,000	35%
Operating Profit/Loss	-$2,473,000	-2%	$69,063,000	8%	$76,594,000	9%
Gain/Loss on disposal of assets	($33,910,000)		($279,751,000)		-$31,440,000	
Other Income	$7,033,000		($1,496,000)		-$1,022,000	
Earnings/Loss before taxes	($29,350,000)		($212,184,000)		$44,132,000	
Income Taxes (Recovery)	$0		($9,932,000)		$29,621,000	
Net Earnings After Tax	($29,350,000)		($202,252,000)		$14,511,000	
Retained Earnings, start of year	($391,144,000)		($126,372,000)		($76,900,000)	
Bonus/Dividends Paid	($2,710,000)		($62,105,000)		($65,005,000)	
Net Earnings After Tax	($29,350,000)		($202,252,000)		$14,511,000	
Retained Earnings, end of year	($423,204,000)		($390,729,000)		($127,394,000)	

KEY RATIOS	SUBJECT	SUBJECT	SUBJECT
PROFITABILITY			
Return on sales	-0.91%	4.84%	5.29%
Return on net worth	0.58%	-17.68%	-60.12%
Return on assets	-0.41%	9.80%	7.93%
Current Ratio	0.67	0.96	1.04
Quick Ratio	1.08	1.16	1.42
Current Liabilities/Net Worth	-77.70%	-78.70%	-243.40%
Current Liabilities/Inventory	206.72%	148.11%	131.00%
Fixed Assets/Net Worth	-152.13%	-175.76%	-352.84%
EFFICIENCY			
Assets/Sales	221.69%	49.37%	66.76%
Sales/Net Working Capital	-1.62	2.65	2.60
Collection Period	73.67	17.81	18.35
Sales/Inventory	1.71	6.87	6.12
Accounts Payable/Sales	0.60	0.18	0.15
Total Liabilities/Net Worth	-142.27%	-180.31%	-758.63%
Tangible Net Worth	($86,078,000)	($78,437,000)	($64,639,000)
Onsite Score 1	-0.22	-0.02	0.01
Onsite Score 2	-0.98	-0.78	-0.18
Onsite Score 3	-0.16	-0.99	0.15
Onsite Score 4	0.45	2.02	1.50
Onsite Score 5	-0.42	-0.33	-0.08
Onsite Risk Score	-1.33	-0.10	1.40

How to make a claim in Small Claims Court (Ontario)

Instructions for Making a Claim

Step 1: COMPLETE the <u>**Plaintiff's Claim**</u> form. Be sure to get the defendant's name right. Explain what happened in detail. Include dates and places. State how much money you want or what goods you want returned. Attach copies of any documents that help your case. Examples are contracts, repair bills and photographs of damaged goods. If you want interest on money you are claiming, ask for it on the claim form. You and the defendant may have a contract that sets an annual interest rate. If so, use that rate. If not, claim the *Courts of Justice Act* interest rate posted on the Ministry of the Attorney General web-site at <u>www.attorneygeneral.jus.gov.on.ca</u>.

If there is more than one plaintiff or defendant, complete an **Additional Parties** form (Form 1A) and put it right behind page one of your plaintiff's claim form. You can get the additional parties form from the court office or at the following website: <u>www.ontariocourtforms.on.ca</u>.

Step 2: **FILE** the plaintiff's claim and related documents by taking it or mailing it to the Small Claims Court office. You must also file a copy for every defendant. There is a fee. Cheques or money orders are payable to the Minister of Finance. The fees are listed at the court office and online at: <u>www.attorneygeneral.jus.gov.on.ca</u>. The clerk will return stamped copies of the plaintiff's claim to you.

Step 3—SERVE. You must deliver a copy of the filed claim and your documents to each defendant. This is called "serving" the defendants. There are rules about how this must be done. See the Small Claims Court **"Guide to Serving Documents"** at the court office or online at <u>www.attorneygeneral.jus.gov.on.ca</u>.

Instructions pour présenter une demande

*Étape 1: REMPLISSEZ la formule **Demande du demandeur**. Assurez-vous d'indiquer le nom du défendeur correctement. Expliquez ce qui s'est passé en détail. Précisez les dates et les lieux. Indiquez la somme d'argent demandée ou les biens dont vous demandez la restitution. Joignez des copies des documents à l'appui de votre cause. Par exemple, des contrats, des factures de réparation et des photographies des biens endommagés. Si vous voulez des intérêts sur la somme demandée, demandez-les sur la formule de demande. Si vous et le défendeur avez conclu un contrat fixant un taux d'intérêt annuel, utilisez ce taux. Sinon, demandez le taux d'intérêt visé par la Loi sur les tribunaux judiciaires qui est affiché sur le site Web du ministère du Procureur général à l'adresse www.attorneygeneral.jus.gov.on.ca.*

*S'il y a plus d'un demandeur ou d'un défendeur, remplissez la formule **Parties additionnelles** (formule 1A) que vous placerez après la première page de votre formule de demande du demandeur. Vous pouvez obtenir la formule sur les parties additionnelles au greffe ou sur le site Web suivant: www.ontariocourtforms.on.ca.*

Étape 2: DÉPOSEZ la demande du demandeur et les documents qui y sont associés en les remettant en personne ou par la poste au bureau de la Cour des petites créances. Vous devez aussi remettre une copie pour chaque défendeur. Cela coûte quelque chose. Les chèques ou mandats doivent être faits à l'ordre du ministre des Finances. Les frais sont publiés au bureau de la Cour des petites créances et en ligne à l'adresse www.attorneygeneral.jus.gov.on.ca. Le greffier vous remettra des copies officialisées de la demande du demandeur.

*Étape 3—SIGNIFIEZ. Vous devez remettre une copie de la demande déposée et de vos documents à chacun des défendeurs. C'est ce qui s'appelle la «signification» aux défendeurs. Il existe des règles sur la façon de signifier. Consultez le **«Guide sur la signification des documents»** de la Cour des petites créances au greffe ou en ligne à l'adresse www.attorneygeneral.jus.gov.on.ca.*

Is it worth it? It is important to consider whether the person or company you are claiming from is likely to be able to pay. If they:

- are unemployed;
- are bankrupt;
- have no money of their own;
- have no personal property and have nothing else of value belonging to them (such as a car) which is not subject to a lease agreement;
- have ceased to carry on business; or
- have other debts to pay,

the court may not be able to help you get your money. However, you may be able to get your money if you are prepared to accept small instalments over a period of time. See the Small Claims Court **"After Judgment—Guide to Getting Results"** at the court office or online at www.attorneygeneral.jus.gov.on.ca.

DO NOT FILE THIS PAGE.

Votre demande en vaut-elle la peine? Il est important de se demander si la personne ou la compagnie à laquelle vous demandez une somme est vraisemblablement en mesure de payer. Si, selon le cas:

- *elle est sans emploi;*
- *elle a fait faillite;*
- *elle n'a pas d'argent à son nom;*
- *elle n'a pas de biens meubles et n'a aucune autre possession de valeur (telle qu'une automobile) qui ne fait pas l'objet d'un contrat de location;*
- *elle a cessé ses activités;*
- *elle a d'autres dettes à payer,*

le tribunal ne sera peut-être pas capable de vous aider à obtenir votre argent. Cependant, vous pourrez peut-être l'obtenir si vous êtes disposé(e) à accepter des petits versements échelonnés. Consultez le «Guide sur la façon d'obtenir des résultats après le jugement» de la Cour des petites créances au greffe ou en ligne à l'adresse www.attorneygeneral.jus.gov.on.ca.

NE DÉPOSEZ PAS LA PRÉSENTE PAGE.

ONTARIO

Superior Court of Justice
Cour supérieure de justice

Plaintiff's Claim
Demande du demandeur

Form / *Formule* 7A Ont. Reg. No. / *Règl. de l'Ont.* : 258/98

Small Claims Court / *Cour des petites créances de*   Claim No. / *N° de la demande*

Seal / *Sceau*

Address / *Adresse*

Phone number / *Numéro de téléphone*

Plaintiff No. 1 / *Demandeur n° 1*   ☐ Additional plaintiff(s) listed on attached Form 1A. *Le ou les demandeurs additionnels sont mentionnés sur la formule 1A ci-jointe.*   ☐ Under 18 years of age. *Moins de 18 ans.*

Last name, or name of company / *Nom de famille ou nom de la compagnie*		
First name / *Premier prénom*	Second name / *Deuxième prénom*	Also known as / *Également connu(e) sous le nom de*
Address (street number, apt., unit) / *Adresse (numéro et rue, app., unité)*		
City/Town / *Cité/ville*	Province	Phone no. / *N° de téléphone*
Postal code / *Code postal*		Fax no. / *N° de télécopieur*
Representative / *Représentant(e)*		LSUC # / *N° du BHC*
Address (street number, apt., unit) / *Adresse (numéro et rue, app., unité)*		
City/Town / *Cité/ville*	Province	Phone no. / *N° de téléphone*
Postal code / *Code postal*		Fax no. / *N° de télécopieur*

Defendant No. 1 / *Défendeur n° 1*   ☐ Additional defendant(s) listed on attached Form 1A. *Le ou les défendeurs additionnels sont mentionnés sur la formule 1A ci-jointe.*   ☐ Under 18 years of age. *Moins de 18 ans.*

Last name, or name of company / *Nom de famille ou nom de la compagnie*		
First name / *Premier prénom*	Second name / *Deuxième prénom*	Also known as / *Également connu(e) sous le nom de*
Address (street number, apt., unit) / *Adresse (numéro et rue, app., unité)*		
City/Town / *Cité/ville*	Province	Phone no. / *N° de téléphone*
Postal code / *Code postal*		Fax no. / *N° de télécopieur*
Representative / *Représentant(e)*		LSUC # / *N° du BHC*
Address (street number, apt., unit) / *Adresse (numéro et rue, app., unité)*		
City/Town / *Cité/ville*	Province	Phone no. / *N° de téléphone*
Postal code / *Code postal*		Fax no. / *N° de télécopieur*

FORM / *FORMULE* 7A   **PAGE 2**

REASONS FOR CLAIM AND DETAILS / *MOTIFS DE LA DEMANDE ET PRÉCISIONS*

Explain what happened, including where and when. Then explain how much money you are claiming or what goods you want returned.

Expliquez ce qui s'est passé, en précisant où et quand. Ensuite indiquez la somme d'argent que vous demandez ou les biens dont vous demandez la restitution, explication à l'appui.

If you are relying on any documents, you **MUST** attach copies to the claim. If evidence is lost or unavailable, you **MUST** explain why it is not attached.

*Si vous vous appuyez sur des documents, vous **DEVEZ** en annexer des copies à la demande. Si une preuve est perdue ou n'est pas disponible, vous **DEVEZ** expliquer pourquoi elle n'est pas annexée.*

What happened?
Where?
When?

Que s'est-il
passé?
Où?
Quand?

Ian Fearon CCE, CCP

FORM / *FORMULE* 7A   PAGE 3

How much? $ ....
Combien?   (Principal amount claimed / *Somme demandée*) $

☐   ADDITIONAL PAGES ARE ATTACHED BECAUSE MORE ROOM WAS NEEDED.
    DES FEUILLES SUPPLÉMENTAIRES SONT ANNEXÉES EN RAISON DU MANQUE D'ESPACE.

The plaintiff also claims pre-judgment interest from ....   under:
Le demandeur demande aussi des intérêts   (Date)   *conformément à :*
antérieurs au jugement de

(Check only   ☐ the *Courts of Justice Act*
one box /   *la* Loi sur les tribunaux judiciaires
Cochez une
seule case)   ☐ an agreement at the rate of ....   % per year
                     un accord au taux de   *% par an*

and post-judgment interest and court costs.
et des intérêts postérieurs au jugement, ainsi que les dépens.

Prepared on: ...., 20 ....   _____
Fait le :   (Signature of plaintiff or representative / *Signature du*
                                                       demandeur/de la demanderesse ou du/de la représentant(e))

Issued on: ...., 20 ....   _____
Délivré le :   (Signature of clerk / *Signature du greffier*)

CAUTION TO DEFENDANT:	**IF YOU DO NOT FILE A DEFENCE** (Form 9A) with the court within twenty (20) calendar days after you have been served with this Plaintiff's Claim, judgment may be obtained without notice and enforced against you. Forms and self-help materials are available at the Small Claims Court and on the following website: www.ontariocourtforms.on.ca.
AVERTISSEMENT AU DÉFENDEUR :	*SI VOUS NE DÉPOSEZ PAS DE DÉFENSE (formule 9A) auprès du tribunal au plus tard vingt (20) jours civils après avoir reçu signification de la présente demande du demandeur, un jugement peut être obtenu sans préavis et être exécuté contre vous. Vous pouvez obtenir les formules et la documentation à l'usage du client à la Cour des petites créances et sur le site Web suivant : www.ontariocourtforms.on.ca.*

Superior Court of Justice
Cour supérieure de justice

Terms of Settlement
Conditions de la transaction

Form / *Formule* 14D Ont. Reg. No. / *Règl. de l'Ont.* : 258/98

_____
Small Claims Court / *Cour des petites créances de*

_____
Claim No. / *N° de la demande*

_____
Address / *Adresse*

_____
Phone number / *Numéro de téléphone*

BETWEEN / *ENTRE*

_____

Plaintiff(s) / *Demandeur(s)/demanderesse(s)*

and / *et*

_____

Defendant(s) / *Défendeur(s)/défenderesse(s)*

We have agreed to settle this action on the following terms:
Nous avons convenu de régler la présente action selon les conditions suivantes :

1. _____ shall pay to
   (Name of party(ies) / *Nom de la ou des parties*)   *verse à*

   _____ the sum of
   (Name of party(ies) / *Nom de la ou des parties*)   *la somme de*

   $ _____ as follows as full and final settlement of the claim, inclusive of interest and costs:
   $ comme suit, à titre de transaction complète et définitive sur la demande, y compris les intérêts et les dépens :

   (Provide terms of payment such as start date, frequency, amount and duration / *Indiquez les modalités de paiement telles que la date de début des versements ainsi que leur fréquence, leur montant et leur durée.*)

Ian Fearon CCE, CCP

FORM / *FORMULE* 14D   **PAGE 2**

Claim No. / *N° de la demande*

2. This claim (and Defendant's Claim, if any) is withdrawn.
Cette demande (et celle du défendeur, le cas échéant) est retirée (sont retirées).

3. If a party to these terms of settlement fails to comply, judgment in the terms of settlement may be obtained against that party on motion to the court or this action may continue as if there has been no settlement.
Si une partie aux présentes conditions de la transaction n'en observe pas les conditions, un jugement suivant les conditions de la transaction peut être obtenu contre cette partie sur présentation d'une motion au tribunal ou la présente action peut continuer comme s'il n'y avait jamais eu de transaction.

4. Provided that the terms of settlement are complied with, the parties above fully and finally release one another from all claims related to the facts and issues raised in this action.
Pourvu que les conditions de la transaction soient observées, les parties susmentionnées se dégagent l'une et l'autre complètement et définitivement de toutes demandes liées aux faits et questions en litige soulevés dans la présente action.

The parties do not need to sign terms of settlement on the same day, but each must sign in the presence of his or her witness who signs a moment later. (For additional parties' signatures, attach a separate sheet in the below format.)
Les parties ne sont pas tenues de signer les conditions de la transaction le même jour, mais chacune doit les signer en présence de son témoin, qui les signe à son tour aussitôt après. (S'il y a lieu, annexez une autre feuille portant la signature des parties additionnelles présentée selon le format indiqué ci-dessous.)

_____, 20 ___

(Signature of party / *Signature de la partie*)

_____

(Name of party / *Nom de la partie*)

_____

(Signature of witness / *Signature du témoin*)

_____

(Name of witness / *Nom du témoin*)

_____, 20 ___

(Signature of party / *Signature de la partie*)

_____

(Name of party / *Nom de la partie*)

_____

(Signature of witness / *Signature du témoin*)

_____

(Name of witness / *Nom du témoin*)

_____, 20 ___

(Signature of party / *Signature de la partie*)

_____

(Name of party / *Nom de la partie*)

_____

(Signature of witness / *Signature du témoin*)

_____

(Name of witness / *Nom du témoin*)

_____, 20 ___

(Signature of party / *Signature de la partie*)

_____

(Name of party / *Nom de la partie*)

_____

(Signature of witness / *Signature du témoin*)

_____

(Name of witness / *Nom du témoin*)

Form 75

Demand for Repossession of Goods

(Paragraph 81.1(1)(a) of the Act)

To: , purchaser (*or* trustee *or* receiver)

I,   , of   (*address*), (*or* as   of   ,) supplier, hereby demand access to and repossession of the goods described below, which were sold and delivered to   , the purchaser, on the dates and in accordance with the terms set out in the attached documents:

(*Attach copies of documents of sale (invoice, delivery slip, etc.) and provide an appropriate description of the goods.*)

Whereas the purchaser is bankrupt (*or* there is a receiver within the meaning of subsection 243(2) of the Act, appointed in respect of the purchaser's property) the trustee (*or* receiver) is required to release the goods described above in accordance with subsection 81.1(1) of the Act.

Dated at   , this   day of   .

                              Supplier

Telephone Number:
Fax Number:
E-mail Address:

NOTE: If a copy of this Form is sent electronically by means such as email, the name and contact information of the sender, prescribed in Form 1.1, must be added at the end of the document.

Putting it all Together; a Case Study

I've covered a lot of topics in this guide, some of which you may never have a need for. I'm sometimes asked if there have been cases where most of my recommendations were implemented and if so what were the results? This case study involved almost all the material in this guide.

I recently completed an 18 month project for a company that I will call "M." When I started working with "M" I knew there were problems in their Credit department and that they needed a lot of help. It wasn't until I started the project that I found out how serious the issues were;

- there was no procedure or policy in place
- more than 30% of the accounts receivable were 90 days past due
- there was a 6 month backlog of more than 500 new credit applications that had not been investigated
- there were more than 5,000 active accounts and only 3 staff to collect the receivables
- some customers who had not paid for more than 2 years were still being allowed to buy product
- credit limits were not being managed and in many cases there was no credit limit at all
- despite profit margins of more than 50%, the company had not made a profit in years
- bad debts were being accrued on a monthly basis but management was reluctant to approve the write offs since it would highlight a lack of controls
- the staff was disinterested in resolving any of the issues
- the owners were trying to recover their investment but didn't have a viable exit strategy

Shortly after I started, I discovered that the company's bank had stopped advancing funds and had issued a three week notice during which the existing loan had to be reduced. No other source of financing was interested in providing funds since the receivables were in such poor shape.

I implemented almost every recommendation in this guide;

- I wrote procedure and policy similar to the one in the index. I included the staff in the process so that they shared ownership
- I retrained the staff on effective collection techniques and made them accountable for their customers
- I ordered credit reports on all 500 accounts and opened them using the guidelines in this manual
- accounts with a balance of less than $150 were outsourced on a contingency basis
- new orders for customers who had not paid for more than 90 days were changed to cash or credit card
- any customer that was over 90 days past due received a 10 day demand letter followed by a third party collection letter
- I implemented a weekly over limit report and held the staff accountable for making sure their accounts were current and within the limit
- I reviewed every account that had been scheduled for bad debt write off and obtained approval to write off all bankrupt accounts and accounts that were no longer in business
- results by staff were posted in the department so that they began to compete among themselves to improve their accounts

At the end of the project, the results spoke for themselves;

- the procedure and policy was shared with the bank which had enough faith in the process to extend the three week notice. The bank loan was eventually paid in full and the company has a mid-6 figure cash balance on hand
- the staff became effective at collecting past due accounts and took pride in improving their aging. They formed working relationships with their customers and improved the aging from 30% over 90 days to less than 4%. My best collector was hired as a supervisor by one of our customers
- the backlog of bad debt write offs was dealt with and more than $125,000 in accruals were returned to income
- the newly opened accounts provided more than $1 million in available credit limits and new accounts are now opened in an average of 2 business days
- 85% of the accounts with a balance under $150 paid their accounts with the help of the outsourcing agent
- more than 90% of the customers that were over 90 days past due paid their account after receiving a demand for payment. The balance was placed for collection with more than 37% paying within the free 10 day demand period
- the weekly credit limit report helped bring accounts current and indentified several pending insolvencies
- the company was able to successfully transition from a corporation to a franchisor allowing the owners to recover much of their investment through future royalties

I don't expect that your results will be this dramatic but if you implement the improvements that I outline in this guide, you will improve your cash flow, increase your profits and grow your business. At the end of the day you can mark your invoices

PAID